Easy Walks near Dublin

Joss Lynam
assisted by
Ruth Lynam

D0279232

Gill & Macmillan Ltd
Hume Avenue, Park West
Dublin 12
with associated companies throughout the world
www.gillmacmillan.ie
© Joss Lynam 1999
0 7171 2789 3
Maps drawn by Justin May
Design by XO Design
Print origination by Carole Lynch
Printed by ColourBooks Ltd, Dublin

This book is typeset in 10/11.5pt Italian Garamond.

Important Note

Every effort has been made to ensure that the text and maps in this
guidebook are correct at time of publication but neither the author
nor the publishers accept any responsibility for errors or omissions.

Furthermore, changes will inevitably take place which will render
portions of this guidebook outdated and incorrect.

If errors are found the publishers will be very pleased to hear
of them.

Contents

A few Dos and Don'ts — mainly for the hill walks

- Always carry some food and (more important) drink
- Always plan to be back before dark
- Do carry a torch in winter
- Do carry a simple first aid box
- Do tell someone where you've gone
- Don't be afraid to turn back if you are tired or the weather turns bad
- Don't walk solo except on frequented paths
- Do check the weather forecast before starting

Thanks

My thanks are due to many organisations and people who helped me to write this book, both wittingly and unwittingly.

Firstly this book could not have been written until the Ordnance Survey published the Discovery Series 1:50,000 scale maps. The old 'half-inch' maps by reason of their small scale could not possibly have included the amount of detail that is needed for these short walks. I have been known to grunt about small errors, but that does not negate the huge debt that all walkers owe to the OS for the rapid and generally efficient publication of this series.

For maps also, I have to thank the orienteers who have mapped the orienteering areas of Dublin and Wicklow. These very detailed maps on scales of 1:10,000 and 1:15,000 have been invaluable on many walks, especially in the woods, where the OS maps, not just because of their smaller scale but because of their cartographical method (aerial survey), cannot pick out the small paths which delight walkers. Perhaps a dozen times I have rummaged in the box that contains the crumpled maps of my orienteering experiences over nearly thirty years to find the one which will help me.

I am greatly indebted to other authors. Most of all, perhaps, to Michael Fewer who has shown me a path of excellence which I have tried, mostly unsuccessfully, to follow. To Keith Collie who knows more about Wicklow than I do and who drew my attention to the attraction of some Dublin public parks I'd overlooked; to David Herman and Jean Boydell whose work on the *Walk Guide East of Ireland* gave me many ideas; and to Seán de Courcy for the history of Bohernabreena.

My deep thanks to Justin May for the sketch maps; we have worked together for so long, and he is so knowledgeable about walking and Wicklow, that he can create exactly the map I require from the worst of photocopied sketches.

In Gill & Macmillan it has always been a pleasure to work with Fergal Tobin who bears my delays patiently, who laughs at my jokes, and who puts up with my constant slagging. My respect and thanks to D Rennison Kunz; over the twenty years of my collaboration with G & M, it has become quite clear to me that she is the glue (if she'll pardon the description) which holds G & M together.

My wife ... Authors' thanks to their wives (or more rarely to their husbands) are a cliché, but in my case it's no cliché. Nora has joined me on some walks, made valuable suggestions, read every description, pointed out the discrepancies, queried the uncertainties, and has not been afraid to argue (and win) her point. This is on top of feeding me, providing tea at all hours, putting up with my working on this book until 11 p.m., driving a second car when needed, and in general, being tolerant far beyond the call of marital duty. (*Actually tolerance has recently broken down: I've been told, quite clearly, that if ever again I have New Year's Day as a deadline, it'll be grounds for divorce.*)

Finally, thanks to my daughter Ruth whose name appears on the title page because of her essential work — as deadlines approached — in checking and writing up those Walks in her West Wicklow bailiwick. Collaboration with her was a pleasure, marred only by the idiosyncrasies of her word processor!

Respect the countryside

- Protect wildlife, plants and trees — do not pick flowers
- Take your litter home with you
- Do not pollute water supplies
- Respect farmland
- Don't interfere with farm animals
- Leave all gates as you find them
- Don't block entrances when parking

Introduction

I am now in my seventy-fifth year and my limbs are complaining strongly about the misuse they have received for the last sixty years on mountains all over the world. So they welcomed the proposal from Fergal Tobin of Gill & Macmillan that I should write a guidebook about walks round Dublin — easy walks — not exceeding three hours in duration. Hence this description of forty walks mostly within an hour's drive of Dublin, all within my now limited capabilities.

Some of the walks included are old favourites that have filled in a summer evening or a winter morning; others are quite new to me, and this is especially true of the walks north of the River Liffey where, as a southsider, I don't venture as often as I should. (*When I asked Fingal County Council to send me information about their parks, and gave my southside address, there came the earnest query — do you realise all these walks are north of the Liffey?*) Anyway, it has been difficult to find walks north and west of Dublin — there simply isn't the terrain where we can walk freely.

South of Dublin and into Wicklow we are fortunate in having plenty of forests owned by Coillte, the Irish Forestry Board, who permit walking in their forests. But it is too easy to pick forest walks; some can be dull because of the predominance of spruce and other coniferous species, of felled areas, and of young trees. Also, of course, what *I* describe as a fine area of mature trees may be a battlefield of piled branches and rutted extraction tracks when *you* get to walk there in a couple of years. Fortunately Coillte are conserving some areas of deciduous trees; these will always make splendid walks. Finally, their forest tracks are often the only means of crossing the pastures and cultivated fields between a public road and the open hillside. Which brings me to the question of ...

Access

When I started walking in Ireland fifty years ago, walkers were a rare species and farming was much less intensive. As a result you could walk nearly anywhere and be sure of a welcome and a chat if you met anyone. Now (and I must take a share of blame) walking is a big and still growing activity, and some farmers have said NO to access: because of vandalism, because of dogs scaring sheep, because simply the big numbers of walkers result in damaged fences, eroded tracks, left-open gates. While I deplore it, I find it difficult to blame them. The wonder is that there remains such goodwill among so many farmers, as can be seen by anyone who works with them on bodies like the Wicklow Uplands Forum, where farmers and 'recreational users' come together to work out how public access and successful farming can cohabit.

I have not knowingly routed any of these walks across private property, except — and this is quite a big exception — on the unfenced mountains, to which traditionally there has been no objection to access. But (outside of the Wicklow National Park) the mountains are all private property; even commonage is private property, though there may be dozens of farmers sharing it. Without access to these hills our walking would be terribly restricted, so, if only for selfish reasons (and I hope for other reasons too), we must respect that private property, realising that the mountains are an important part of the farming industry — yes it's an industry now — which we must not damage. Chiefly that means not frightening sheep and that means NO DOGS on the hill walks. Dogs are man's best friend — but the sheep's worst enemy. Look at it from your dog's point of view: a farmer is legally entitled to shoot any dog he sees annoying sheep; very few farmers enjoy shooting dogs, but sometimes they have to do it. Why put your dog at risk?

After that fierce homily I hope I haven't dissuaded you from walking the hills. Give a little thought for the farmer, and you have the freedom of the hills.

You will find a list of environmental Dos and Don'ts in the box on page vi. In a box on page xv I've listed the walks where I suggest you shouldn't take dogs — it's only half of the forty.

One of my aims in writing this book is to help Dublin people (and others) who are not walkers to start that activity. So I have been almost pedantic in my descriptions of how to follow each walk and then sugar-coated the dull pill of 'turn left, turn right' with bits of history, natural history and even personal experiences. All except the longer walks are suitable for families. I have also tried wherever possible to choose walks that are circular and that can be reached by public transport. The latter have the advantage that they are often less dependent on circularity. I have used the term 'car' for private transport, but a bicycle will go wherever a car will, and often a bit further.

I hope that this book will also be useful to visitors from the rest of Ireland and from abroad. There are many, surely, who are not serious walkers but would enjoy a short walk or two and, as strangers, may appreciate the detail I have given here.

Finally, I hope this book may stimulate people like myself, whose best walking days are over, to keep active, and even if they hang up their boots, at least to keep going in trainers!

If you are already an experienced walker, you can ignore the next section!

Maps and Navigation

The minimum that anyone who uses this book needs is some kind of a road map in order to find the walks. You may already have a road map, but if you haven't I suggest the Ordnance Survey 1:250,000 (¼ inch to 1 mile) map 'East', because it will also help you to pick out the mountains mentioned in summit views. The sketch maps which accompany each walk are all you need, with the text, to guide you round many of them, particularly the low-level ones, but when tackling the longer walks on the 'Middle' and 'Big' Hills I do suggest that you carry the OS Discovery 1:50,000 (1¼ inches to 1 mile) maps. They are not difficult to read, they can obviously tell you a lot more about your surroundings than the small sketch maps can, and are very useful if by chance you stray from the route. The cost is not high — two Sheets (50 and 56) cover ninety per cent of the walks. To preserve your map (and this guidebook!) carry them in a plastic bag, or a map case.

On some of the mountain walks where you might run into mist, I have suggested you carry a compass, but even on these walks no accurate compass work is involved. I hope, however, that, when you have worked through a selection of walks in this book, some of you may be tempted to bigger things, and that you will be able to explore safely the hills, woods and watersides of Ireland.

I have used the metric system for heights and distances; all our modern maps are metric, even our road signs are going metric.

Timing

I have taken the risk of suggesting how long a walk might take you, so I had better explain my method. I am assuming that you can cover a kilometre in somewhere between fifteen and twenty minutes on the flat, depending on the surface on which you are walking, and that every 100 m of height gained will take an extra fifteen minutes. So a walk of 6 km with a climb of 200 m will take ninety minutes for the flat walk plus thirty minutes for the ascent — total two hours. If the going was very rough on half the walk I might add an extra quarter-hour. Time yourself on a couple of walks to find out whether you are faster or slower than the times I give, and plan accordingly. Please remember that the times given do not allow for any rests or stops of more than a couple of minutes. Especially in the winter when the days are short, it is important to make sure that you can finish your planned walk well before dark.

Clothing and Equipment

I have given some suggestions on equipment. Everybody owns trainers (or walking shoes) and for many walks either are perfectly adequate. Boots are recommended if the going is very rough, muddy or boggy — wet feet are unpleasant, especially in winter.

One of the advantages of the Irish climate is its changeability; if it's raining now, it may be fine soon. But the converse is equally true, so it is generally unwise to go walking without protection against rain. *I mean appropriate protection — I have a friend who swears by an umbrella, but he rock-climbs in toeless sandals and I don't recommend that either.* Most of us possess a light anorak — that will suffice on many walks, as mostly will a plastic mackintosh. If I think greater protection is required — against strong winds and low temperatures — I mention 'weather gear', by which I mean a 'fleece' or extra sweater, and perhaps a woolly cap and gloves as well as windproof rain gear. As you go higher, it gets colder, wetter and windier. On the summits of the two big mountains in this book — Mullaghcleevaun (Walk 30) and Tonelagee (Walk 32) — it is between 6 and 8 °Celsius colder than at sea level; the wind is twice as strong, and the annual rainfall is more than double that in Dublin. So be sure that you are well prepared on such walks. On the other hand if you choose a warm summer day with a good forecast for your walk, then such precautions can be considerably scaled down.

Walking sticks. My arthritic knees remind me whenever I walk downhill that I should have taken to using a pair of walking sticks long before I did. I know it looks silly to be walking over the Little Sugar Loaf using a pair of adjustable ski sticks, but, please believe me, the comfort in descent is worth the embarrassment and the silly jibes about 'are you expecting snow?' If you get the chance, borrow a pair to try out — you'll be surprised how helpful they are. Being collapsible they can easily be stowed away before reaching tarmac. I have suggested a stick (or a pair!) where the ground or path is very rough.

Anything that you carry, as opposed to wear, can most easily be carried in a small rucksack — a 'day sack' in technical terms.

I have occasionally suggested carrying books on birds and plants, and a pair of binoculars, for special walks, but in fact they are worth taking on nearly *all* the walks.

I always carry a camera. The modern compact with a zoom lens from 35 mm to 70 mm or 80 mm is light, adaptable and easy to use. It can be hung around your neck, ready for action when the cloud fleetingly clears the hilltop, or the setting sun blazes red, or the geese suddenly take off. It will also record the autumn colours of the leaves, the spring blossoms, the purple heather and yellow gorse — and of course your companions!

I hope that the long list of items to wear or carry won't put you off. It is impossible to cater for all occasions and while I don't want you to perspire on the Royal Canal in fleece, anorak and balaclava, I certainly don't want you to freeze on Tonelagee in tee-shirt and shorts. In the end, it is up to you to use a little common sense. Don't rush out and buy a lot of gear. Start with the walks that need only what you already possess, and work up. There are shops for walking gear, in Dublin and other towns, where you can get good gear — and good advice. Remember that you can take off a layer if you are too hot, but there is no easy remedy if you are too cold.

Finally I had better say that in the very unlikely event of your needing rescue, there are two highly efficient Mountain Rescue teams in the Dublin–Wicklow area — call 999.

For a few simple safety Dos and Don'ts see the box on page iv.

I've enjoyed walking for six decades, and I hope to go on doing so for another few years (a decade is too much to hope). I've enjoyed the research for this book, and I hope you will enjoy using it. Good walking!

Joss Lynam
31 December 1998

Some Other Walks

The forty walks described are not the only options round Dublin. The public parks (pages 122–7) offer good and varied short walks — all in reach of public transport. Beaches have good possibilities. North Dublin especially offers good walks on the coast at Donabate; either walk north from the martello tower at Donabate to its twin at Portrane, or south along Portmarnock beach to the mouth of the Broadmeadow Estuary. Every Dubliner knows Sandymount Strand, but visitors may not. Killiney Beach is another pleasant walk.

Dubliners have long been countering the effects of festivities by breezy morning walks along Dun Laoghaire West Pier, or the South Wall of the Liffey, a particularly good walk, waves beating on either side of the narrow causeway, fine views across Dublin Bay to Howth Head, and a close-up of the shipping using the Port.

Coillte's 'Open Forest' policy suggests further opportunities. The Discovery maps I've recommended will show you other forests you might explore — Kilmashogue near Marlay Park, Saggart out to the west, Ballynahinch near Newtownmountkennedy, Carrick near the Devil's Glen.

Obviously you can walk other sections of the Grand and Royal Canals: the Leinster Aqueduct across the Liffey on the Grand near Sallins, and the deep cutting on the Royal near Blanchardstown are of special interest.

There is a good walk on the bank of the River Boyne near Slane. And on the River Liffey the section by the Coronation Plantation below Sally Gap makes a pleasant walk, as does the stretch at the entry to the Pollaphuca Reservoir.

See the Bibliography for some other guidebooks.

The Walks by Duration

One Hour or Less

Two Hours or Less, but More than One Hour

Over Two Hours

The Walks by Character

Note: Many walks will come into two categories. The Devil's Glen is a riverside walk in a wooded valley; the access to many of the mountains (Maulin for instance) is through forestry. Walks falling into two categories are starred (*).

Coast

Howth Head Cliff Path, p. 9
The North Bull Island, p. 15

Bray Head, p. 59*
Greystones Cliff Path, p. 76

Rivers, Canals, Lakes

The Boyne Towpath — Oldbridge, p. 2*
Ward River Linear Park, p. 6
Royal Canal — Leixlip to Maynooth, p. 18
Grand Canal — Milltown Feeder, p. 21
The Bohernabreena Reservoirs, p. 27

The Dargle Gorge, p. 54*
Upper and Lower Lough Bray, p. 56*
Russelstown Wood, p. 79*
The Vartry Reservoirs, p. 91
The Devil's Glen, p. 100*
The Vale of Clara, p. 110

Woods

Dalkey and Killiney Hill, p. 24*
Three Rock, Fairy Castle and Two Rock Mountains, p. 30*
Tibradden Mountain, p. 33*
The Massey Woods, p. 36
The Hellfire Club, p. 36*
Carrickgollogan, p. 39*
The Scalp, p. 42*
Seahan, p. 45*
Ravens Rock and Prince William's Seat, p. 48*
Cloghleagh Wood, p. 51

The Dargle Gorge, p. 54*
Maulin, p. 67*
Russelstown Wood, p. 79*
The J.B. Malone Memorial from Ballinastoe, p. 85*
The Devil's Glen, p. 100*
'Little' Brockagh, p. 104*
Derrybawn Mountain, p. 107*
The Vale of Clara, p. 110*
Deputy's Pass, p. 113
Keadeen Mountain, p. 119*

Small Hills

Middle Hills

Big Hills

**Please don't take a dog on these walks (birds and other
wildlife, sheep, regulations):
Numbers 5, 7, 10, 11, 15, 16, 19 (long), 21, 23, 24, 25,
28, 29, 30, 32, 33, 35, 36, 39, 40**

The Walks Accessible by Public Transport

The following walks can be done reasonably easily using public transport. I haven't included those which are served by perhaps one passing bus a day. The details of the suitable bus or train are included in the walk description. Do take care to study timetables in advance, and remember that Sunday timetables are often skimpier than weekday ones. The contact addresses and phone numbers are:

Iarnród Éireann (Irish Rail) (main line and DART services)
Connolly Station, Dublin 1. Tel: 353 (0)1 836 6222

Bus Átha Cliath (Dublin Bus) (Dublin area)
59 Upper O'Connell Street, Dublin 1. Tel: 353 (0)1 873 4222

Bus Éireann (Country buses)
Central Bus Station, Store Street, Dublin 1. Tel: 353 (0)1 836 6111

St Kevin's Bus Service (Dublin–Glendalough)
Roundwood, Co. Wicklow. Tel: 353 (0)1 281 8119

Half an Hour or Less Extra Walking:

Ward River Linear Park, p. 6
Howth Head Cliff Path, p. 9
The Ben of Howth, p. 12
The North Bull Island, p. 15
Royal Canal — Leixlip to Maynooth, p. 18
Dalkey and Killiney Hill, p. 24
Three Rock, Fairy Castle and Two Rock Mountains, p. 30
The Scalp, p. 42

The Dargle Gorge, p. 54
Bray Head, p. 59
The Little Sugar Loaf, p. 64
The Great Sugar Loaf (long only), p. 73
Greystones Cliff Path, p. 76
The Vartry Reservoirs, p. 91
'Little' Brockagh, p. 104
Derrybawn Mountain, p. 107

Over Half an Hour Extra Walking:

Tibradden Mountain, p. 33
Carrickgollogan, p. 39

Carrigoona – Rocky Valley, p. 62

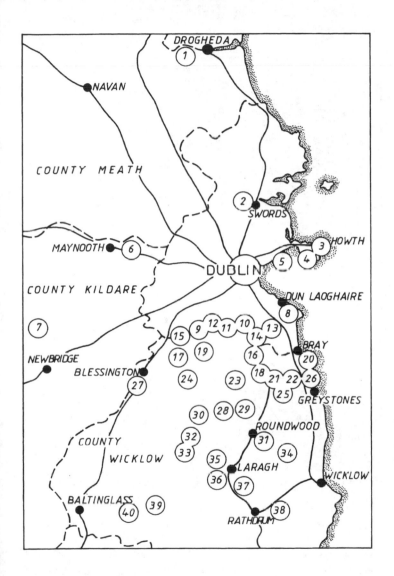

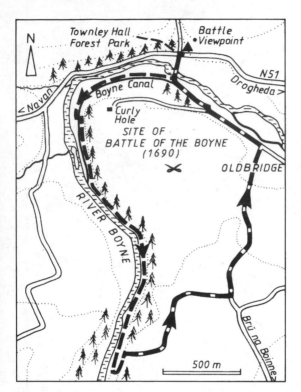

Distance: 6 km
Ascent: 30 m
Time: 1¾ to 2 hours
Equipment: OS Discovery Sheet 43. Trainers (summer), boots (winter).

The Boyne Valley, from Navan to Drogheda, is perhaps the most beautiful, varied and interesting lowland valley in Ireland. You can find meadows, cornfields, steep, wooded slopes, reed banks, castles, the Newgrange complex, the site of the Battle of the Boyne, smooth, calm flow, swirling eddies, weirs and a canal. My difficulty is to pick a stretch which fits the parameters of this book. The difficulty is increased because this is a walk I'd never tried before preparing this book. Yes, I've followed the Boyne from Navan to Drogheda, but in a kayak — a method which does not tell you much about the walking possibilities! I picked the stretch upstream from Oldbridge which is as interesting as any, and which has the advantage of providing a circular walk, even if this does involve some road walking on the return leg. The towpath is rather muddy in places, as is the farm track leading back up to the public road — hence the suggestion of boots, though I walked it in trainers.

From Dublin follow the N1/M1 to Drogheda. As you enter the town, keep to the road signposted Belfast which avoids the town centre. Just after you cross the Boyne, turn left along the N51, signposted Slanc/Navan. Four kilometres along this road you pass a huge sign on the left, 'Battle of the Boyne', and immediately beyond it a car park on the right, just beside a crossroads. Park here. There's a Battle of the Boyne Information Centre beside the car park, but I don't guarantee it will be open.

Before you start walking it is worth climbing up the stepped path behind the car park to the battle viewing point; it is only a very short distance and there's a map to show you the important sites of the battle. Directly below you is the site of the ford where the Williamite cavalry crossed. You can also see some of the walk, though trees hide much of it. The return route of the walk is down the road from the hill opposite.

Now to start the walk itself. Cross the main road and take the road over the impressive lattice girder bridge. You are warned not to cross it if you weigh more than five tons and not to attempt to swim in the river, which is deep and has a strong current — there are impressive swirls and rapids, especially when the river is high. Just beyond the bridge turn right off the road onto a track beside the canal. The Boyne was canalised in the eighteenth century: short sections of canal with locks bypassing the rapids or weirs. It was never a commercial success and has been out of use for many years, but much of the towpath is intact and there is every hope that in a few years it will be possible to walk unhindered from Drogheda to Navan.

The canal presents a surface of green algae, but beyond it are the woods of the Oldbridge demesne, with many fine trees: oak,

3

sycamore, imported cypresses and redwoods. This is good fishing territory and there are little paths with stiles leading off the towpath down to the river.

The towpath crosses to the south bank of the canal by a typical hump-back bridge. There was a lock here, but now the water levels are maintained by a concrete wall under the bridge with a sluice. After the bridge the roar of water indicates the nearness of the river and of a weir and soon you emerge onto open ground where the canal rejoins the river above an old weir. Here you find the first of a series of pillboxes, built during the Second World War — was someone expecting another Williamite invasion?

The towpath continues beside the river, with the demesne woods rising steeply on the left (more exotics — rhododendrons and bamboos!) while across the river are reed beds and water meadows backed by wooded slopes. I saw cormorants on the river; it seems to be quite a recent phenomenon that they come inland. Their numbers increased enormously when the European Union gave them protected status.

You pass a milestone — four miles from Drogheda — and the steep, wooded slopes begin to get higher and close in. A narrow track continues along the bank but the main track rises to an open area (there is a fine set of wooden steps down to the river and a huge sign announces that the fishing is private to the Slane Club) and turns back, climbing steeply to the ruins of a country house. The track improves and winds between fields — stubble when I saw them, but judging by the big bales of straw, there had been a good crop. There is an attractive prospect across the open fields and a fine house — Townley Hall, I think — can be seen on the high ground north of the river. A kilometre or so brings you to a hamlet and the public road.

Turn left down the minor road (I met only one car but it is narrow so keep to the verge) and turn left again at the T-junction. You are now back beside the canal, and this road follows the line of the old towpath. The canal is almost hidden by drooping trees and shrubs. Shortly you meet the impressive gates to the old demesne which the OS map labels, rather curiously, 'Curly Hole'. The road swings sharply right, crosses the canal and continues on the north bank back to the lattice bridge and the car park. When I walked there the autumn colours of the trees on the south bank of the canal were magnificent.

Once you've arrived at the Boyne, of course, there are plenty of other attractions. There are signposts directing you to various parts of the Battle of the Boyne, but nothing is actually visible. On the other hand there is plenty to see — and well worth seeing — at the Boyne Interpretative Centre, with Newgrange and the adjoining monuments. (By the time you read this there may be a through path from the Interpretative Centre to Oldbridge, a good walk if you can muster two cars or an extra bicycle.)

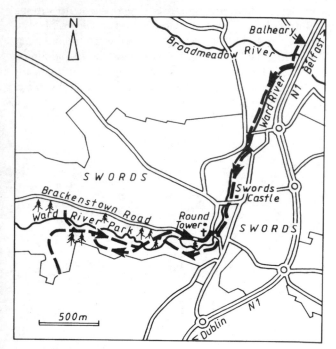

Distance: 7 to 8 km
Ascent: Minimal
Time: 2 hours
Equipment: OS Discovery Sheet 50 or OS Dublin Street Guide. Trainers.

This is a rather different walk to any other in this book because it is an urban walk: but not, I believe, the less enjoyable for that. It was only by chance that I found it while browsing through the Street Guide, and I suspect it is little known except to local people. I don't think it is often walked from end to end, and when I did it one bright, cold, winter Sunday morning I was the only walker without a dog! You are never out of sight of houses, but apart from crossing three roads you are on a footpath all the way, and generally in parkland or woodland. It is also remarkably free from rubbish. Dublin County Council and its successor

Fingal County Council are due much praise for creating this walk, which has added interest from Swords' importance in history. I will describe it using a car, starting from the north end at Balheary and returning there; but there are several possible variations, and it is easily done using public transport. The distance and time shown above are for the complete circuit I have described; knock off half an hour if you stop at Swords on the way back.

Take the Belfast road (N1/M1) from Dublin, past the Airport. Take the bypass around Swords and a short distance beyond the fourth (and last) roundabout there is a left turn, signposted to the Balheary Golf Club and the Emmaus Retreat Centre. A few metres down this road is a car park: well, perhaps there is a car park, although when I walked this route recently the entrance had been blocked with boulders. Hopefully it will be reopened, but even if it isn't, there is plenty of room for three cars between the road and the car park entrance. There is a number 33 bus stop about 200 m on the Swords side of the junction.

Walk through the car park, cross the bridge over the Broadmeadow River (a twin arch which carried the old main road to the north) and turn right onto a path through parkland beside the Ward River. The river has been tamed between straight banks, but in winter at least it has a lively flow. An old, humped arch bridge crosses the river, and you can choose which side to walk. The east side has playing fields, the west has a factory close by but it is well shielded by a belt of trees. What can't be kept out is the hum of traffic on the N1.

Cross a road, enter a grassy area at a gap in the wall, exit through another, and a few metres brings you to a fenced path on the left which crosses to the east (right) bank of the river and continues through parkland to Swords Castle. It's a fine-looking castle, with towers and curtain walls; from 1200 up to the Reformation (about 1540) it was a seat of the Archbishops of Dublin, whose manorial estates here totalled nearly 17,000 hectares. Restoration is in progress and the Constable's Tower is open to the public.

Cross a second road, go through the car park of a small shopping mall and you will find the path on the right (east) bank squeezed between the river and a very urban wall. Across the river, through the trees you can glimpse a round tower, a square tower and a small church — more of them later. When you meet the third road, turn left, keep right at the fork, and turn into the car park on the right. A well-trampled track across the grass leads to a hedge and the main part of the park. The 'official' entrance comes in from the centre of Swords on your left and could be used to start or finish your walk.

Now you are in a very pleasant open park, extending across a flat plain through which the Ward River meanders. The steep valley sides are thickly wooded and at intervals paths lead up to entrances from various housing estates. The main path crosses to the north (left) bank, dives into woodland and emerges to cross the river again back into parkland. You can make a loop here, rising upon the south slope to survey the valley below, before dropping back to the valley floor and a variety of possible paths which I leave you to explore.

You could finish your walk here. A path beyond the end of the loop crosses the river by a bridge with impressive steel fencing and leads up to Brackenstown Road and the number 41X bus (the service is rather infrequent — check the timetable!). I returned by the way I had come, but did not return across the first bridge. Instead I went straight on along a path which brought me out onto that same Brackenstown Road, but much closer to Swords and just near the round tower. I went to explore this and met the verger polishing his front door brass. He told me that while the church dated back only to 1817, the square tower was of twelfth-century date, part of a monastery which had long since disappeared, while the round tower dated back to the ninth century. The original monastery was founded by St Columba; the first abbot was St Finian, who was reputedly a leper — there was once a leper hospital on the nearby 'Spital Hill'. On 9 June 1997 they celebrated the 1,400th anniversary of the monastery's foundation. The square tower is open occasionally and would make a fine viewpoint.

Descend towards the bridge and you will immediately recognise your outward route, which you can follow back to Balheary. Alternatively, continue straight on from the bridge into Swords for a bus or refreshment.

Note: The whole of this walk is passable by wheelchair, except the 'unofficial' entrance to the main park.

3. Howth Head
Cliff Path

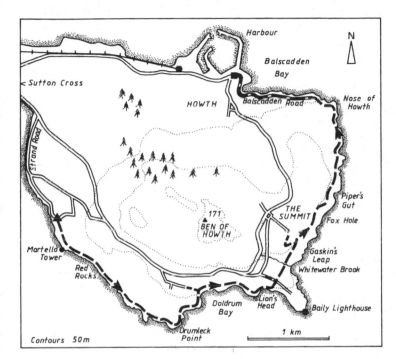

Distance: 7.5 km
Ascent: 120 m
Time: 2¼ to 2½ hours
Equipment: OS Discovery Sheet 50 or OS Dublin Street Guide. Trainers.

This is a fine cliff walk, quite varied, with no steep rises or falls. The path is mostly good though there are rough places and it is a little overgrown in high summer. There is some superb cliff scenery. It is ideally suited for approach by public transport, which, since it isn't a circular walk, is the best answer. It is busy at sunny weekends, expecially with Howth dog exercisers. It has the final advantage that there are at least three places you can leave it en route. It was laid out in the last century by the Great Northern Railway as a tourist amenity, and the occasional old stone seat or pillar can still be seen.

9

Take the number 31A bus from Abbey Street (or else pick it up at Sutton Cross after travelling to Sutton by DART) and get off at the far end of Strand Road in Sutton. The start of the walk is plain, just where Strand Road leaves the sea and becomes Sheilmartin Road.

It starts as a broad, flat path and takes you past a martello tower (a lookout dating to the fear of a French invasion during the Napoleonic wars). Once past the tower the path narrows, and cliffs appear. However, the official notice 'No Through Route' is a definite over-statement, only true for those over eighty, under three, or with a wooden leg. So continue across the hillside which is steep and rocky but perfectly safe. Once you reach Red Rocks, with a very rough pier of boulders providing a small sheltered beach, there are no more difficulties. The walk round Drumleck Point, past Doldrum Bay and Lion's Head, is the most spectacular part of the walk. Coves, secluded beaches, cliffs, rocky islands and pinnacles crowned with waiting cormorants — all these you have, and without danger or difficulty. Note the curious boundary wall on the shore side, its mortar full of mussel shells, and near Drumleck Head the wooden post marking a submarine telegraph cable in the sea bed below. Notice also two concrete bathing pools, built by the Jameson family of distillers, which are the first examples of Portland Cement concrete in Ireland. Above Doldrum Bay you pass close to a high privet hedge on the landward side. Immediately beyond, a path goes left to Ceanchor Road and a bus route, if you so desire. As far as here, it is mostly possible to find paths open to the public leading down to the beaches. Beyond there are still occasional paths, but they have gates and intimidating 'Private' notices.

In other words, you are getting into a more inhabited area, and the path is generally creeping along between a thick hedge which prevents you staring at the inhabitants and the cliff edge masked by another hedge which blocks your view to seaward. On the plus side, the hedges are frequently decorated with exotic blooms; you often walk below an arch of fine garden-escape shrubs (among them the delightfully named 'Hottentot fig', *Carpobrotus edulis*) and at intervals there are breaks which give you views of the wonderful cliff scenery and, on all but the calmest day, surf breaking on the rocks. After passing a house precariously perched to *seaward* of the path (a local assured me the 'foundations are very deep') you suddenly emerge onto open ground in sight of the Baily lighthouse on the very tip of the peninsula. The lighthouse road offers another escape route. So far you have been walking the south side, looking across Dublin Bay to Dun Laoghaire and the Wicklow Mountains beyond. It will be a rare day when you don't see ships heading into or out of Dublin Port, the latest high-speed ferries on their way to and from Holyhead or a scatter of sails of racing yachts.

To continue, turn left onto the road and almost immediately turn right along a continuation of the path. Just here are a couple of large blocks of granite, unexpected since Howth Head is composed entirely of quartzite and there is no geological record of naturally occurring granite anywhere near. On a high embankment you cross the ravine of the Whitewater Brook, a good place to pause to look at the lighthouse and the cliffs of this east face of the Head. Next you find a succession of paths going uphill to the left; they all lead to Howth Summit, another escape route, this time with the added lure of refreshments. Even if you are determined to finish the complete walk, there's nothing to stop you nipping up for a drink and then dropping down by another path to rejoin the Cliff Walk.

The remainder of the Walk as far as Balscadden Bay is a complete contrast to the first part. No more houses, no more trees or shrubs, just a path rising and falling across the slopes above the cliffs, colourful with bell heather, gorse and even some blackberries in season. The cliffs are just as fine, and the waves beat more fiercely, although the path is higher and so the views are more distant and less immediate. But this bit of the walk is not dull, and it certainly has a history, judging by the names — Fox Hole, Piper's Gut, Gaskin's Leap. There are some good names inland as well; I'd love to have brought you down Cowbooter Lane, but I couldn't fit it in.

As you come to the Nose of Howth and turn west, Ireland's Eye, two rocky stacks, come into view with Lambay behind, then the coast of Fingal County and unless lost in haze or mist, the Mountains of Mourne. ('Eye' by the way is simply from the Norse 'iyot', an island.) As the path descends to Balscadden Road, look back at the 'Danger Cliffs' sign and note the man walking determinedly over the edge — could this be Gaskin? Now there remains about 1 km of road walking to Howth, which is a bustling fishing and yachting harbour with a wide variety of pubs, cafés and restaurants, not forgetting bus and DART services back to Dublin.

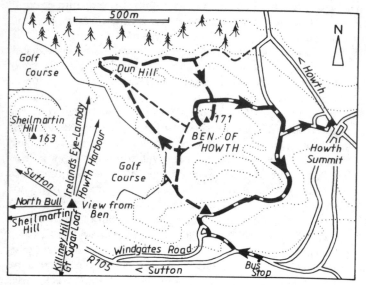

Distance: 3 km
Ascent: 60 m
Time: 1 hour
Equipment: OS Discovery Sheet 50. Trainers.

Walk 3 took us round the perimeter of Howth Head; this walk takes us right into the hilly centre. I'd like to say mountainous, but there is no way that I can classify a high point of 171 m as a mountain; though truly it is a miniature mountain of heather, gorse and rock. As a walk it has everything going for it. Easy access by car or bus, minimal climbing, good paths, wonderful 360° views. Does this sound too easy for the seasoned walker? Easy, yes, but still a great walk not to be missed.

Take the Howth Road (R105) out of Dublin, fork right at Sutton Cross and follow the road (Carrickbrack Road) round the eastern and southern slopes of the Head. At about 3.5 km from the Cross a narrow road (Windgates Road) forks steeply uphill to the left. Follow

12

it twisting left and right and, as it levels out, park in a lay-by beside a gated track entrance on the left (there's room for about five cars).

If using public transport the 31B bus takes you along Carrickbrack Road (I've marked on the sketch map the bus stop where you get out). Walk back a short way, cross the road and walk up the turning on your right. In a few minutes you join Windgates Road and a few more bring you to the start.

Go round the gate and walk the track between high heather and gorse — wonderful colours from spring through to autumn. After only a minute or two you are above the houses and views open up across Dublin Bay, generally busy with shipping, to Killiney Hill (Walk 8) and the Wicklow Mountains. At the first junction go right, then keep left at a rather vague fork. By now you are up on rolling moorland; to your left is cairned Sheilmartin Hill and separated from it by the bright green of one of Howth's two golf courses is Dun Hill, rocky this one, and your next target.

Soon you come to a crossing of tracks. Before going further, just check your position: on your right are three radio masts. The furthest away and biggest sits on top of the Ben of Howth. An eyesore, but a useful one! The Head is a mass of tracks and if you don't like my itinerary you can pick your own, in the knowledge that you will rarely be out of sight of the mast on the Ben, a sure landmark.

At the crossing turn left along a track which runs near the edge of the golf course (close to the sixth tee and what looks to me, a non-player, like an awesome rough) and then curves right to join the track along the ridge which runs from the Ben to Dun Hill. You reach its top by an easy slope, but the other three sides are steep, so that in spite of its meagre height (160 m) it is from here that you get the 360° panorama that I promised you. To the south-west the Wicklow Mountains appear over Sheilmartin Hill, then working clockwise the North Bull (Walk 5), the Sutton isthmus and all Dublin are laid out below you, almost an aerial view. Howth Castle is visible among the trees, then Howth Harbour with its crowds of fishing boats and yachts, backed by Ireland's Eye and its great stacks with Lambay sprawling behind. Finally, in the gap between the Ben and Sheilmartin Hill, Dublin Bay, Killiney Hill and the Great Sugar Loaf (Walk 25) are clear. The summit on which you are standing is actually a burial cairn, and the small hollow among the stones is probably all that remains of the burial chamber.

On the west side of the hill a track contouring along the slope is visible. Descend to it by a little path — it's steep, but very short — and turn right. Follow this track, swinging between rocky knolls among heather and gorse until you reach a junction where you turn back very sharply onto a track which delivers you to the foot of the Ben and a tarmac road.

Go left along the tarmac for some 50 m, then right into an open turning area, on the far side of which are some steps made of railway sleepers; these mark the start of a steep little path to the top of the Ben, disfigured, as I remarked before, by a big radio mast. There is not much to see that you haven't already seen from Dun Hill, but it is the highest point so you can hardly give it a miss. Descend by the way you came, or if you think it a bit steep, a little to your left a wide track swings round to the far (west) side of the Ben to join the tarmac road. Whichever descent you've taken, follow the tarmac road out to the public road, past quarries and a small 'Peace Park'. Turn right back towards your car.

Here the bus user has the advantage; not much more than 100 m along the road, take a left turn which leads directly to Howth Summit, with buses (numbers 31 and 31B) — and a pub and café! Car users must walk back the 600 m or so to their car before sampling the refreshments at the Summit.

Anyone wanting a rather longer walk could start from Howth and follow Walk 3 in reverse as far as the 'escape route' near the Baily lighthouse. Walk up this to Thormanby Road, turn left and very soon you pick up the route from the 31B bus stop to the start. This adds about 1¼ hours to the walking time.

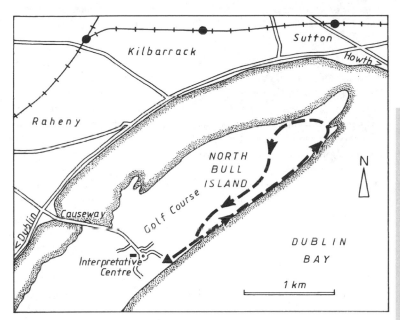

Distance: 5 km
Ascent: Minimal
Time: 1½ hours (plus viewing time!)
Equipment: OS Discovery Sheet 50 or OS Dublin Street Guide. Trainers, binoculars, bird and flower books.

The North Bull Island is a fairly new addition to Ireland; it only began to appear in the eighteenth century and it was really the building first of the South Wall and then of the Bull Wall which created the tidal currents which caused the deposition of sand. The building of the Causeway in 1976 is making for further changes. The Bull is a UNESCO Biosphere Reserve so this is primarily a nature walk, for its rich and varied flora in summer and its unparalleled population of waders and wildfowl in winter (more than twenty thousand birds each November–December). Which do you want to see? Perhaps walk it twice? But everyone will find something to enjoy there, with the fine views across Dublin Bay and the movement of ships in and out of the Port. For the best view of the birds, go there a bit above half-tide: at low tide they are far away at the edge of the mud-flats, at high tide they may be roosting. (Any serious student of flora or birds should try to find the study of the natural history of the North Bull published by the Royal Dublin Society in 1977, ISBN 0 86027 001 7 or 002 5.)

Take the coastal Howth Road out of Dublin; after passing Dollymount and St Anne's Park, turn right at traffic lights and cross the Causeway to the Island. Coming or going, you should stop for what may be your nearest view of the waders — dunlin, knot, redshank, bar-tailed godwit, oystercatcher and grey plover, to name the most common. Once on the Island, take the first turn out of the roundabout which will bring you down to the beach and good parking on hard sand. (It may be worth your while to go first to the Interpretative Centre for more information than I have space to give.)

Set off northward along the hard sand of this spacious strand. For some distance — until you reach a line of boulders extending down to low tide — you are at risk from joy-riding motorists, but beyond the boulders all is peaceful. At the water's edge there are gulls and the ubiquitous oystercatchers; you may also see a cormorant or a shag. On the shore side the first range of dunes is colonised first by sand sedge (*Carex arenaria*) and then by marram grass (*Ammophila arenaria*). You would need to go further into the dunes to find a richer flora. Looking out to sea there is a fine view of the cusps of Dublin Bay, Howth Head (Walks 3 and 4) to the north, and Dalkey (Walk 8) to the south, with generally some shipping in view — perhaps a HSS with its huge following wave.

It is fast, easy walking with the dunes beside you; as you near the end of the Bull, some quirk of current has deposited masses of old shells, making a continuous crackle under your feet. You meet a rather bedraggled wire fence requesting you to keep out because of shore birds (little terns) nesting. Turn left and follow it over the dunes. (There is sometimes a flock of red mergansers at this end of the Bull.)

The path beside the fence leads you down to the inner shore of the island and after a short stretch of beach to a path along the inshore edge of the salt marsh. Now is the time to get out your binoculars and cock your ears to try to distinguish individual calls from the medley of bird noise — curlews at least will be distinctive. Curlews, incidentally, along with mallard, oystercatchers and cormorants, are among the few species to be found here throughout the year; almost all the others spend the summer breeding further north, and either winter in Ireland or stop off for a couple of weeks on their way to winter further south and on their way back north. I've mentioned the waders but there are also plenty of ducks — wigeon, pintail, shelduck, shovelers and teal. Finally there is the grandest of them all — the stately brent-goose. The geese and the grazing ducks are easier to see than the mud-flat feeders — on the marsh they are closer to you; but please don't go too close and disturb them.

Paths proliferate; I suggest you mostly keep close to the edge of the marsh. At neap tides the water hardly touches the marsh but it may be covered completely at a high spring tide. Notable plants are, inward from the sea, glasswort (*Salicornia sp.*) with its striking autumn russet colour, the grass *Puccinellia maritima*, thrift (*Armeria maritima*), a mass of pale pink flowers in June, and beside the path, rushes (*Juncus sp.*). You can venture safely onto the salt marsh, but perhaps rubber boots would be advisable. To your left, just in front of the dunes is a 'dune slack' with alders and willows.

A building is now in sight — the clubhouse of St Anne's Golf Club — and soon you meet the wire mesh fence of the golf course which forces you inland. It is unfortunate that golfers and birds share the same ecological requirements! Plenty of paths here, all rather dull, so as soon as you get bored, cross the dunes back to the strand and so to your car. In the dunes you should meet a wide variety of flowering plants, including several orchids, notably the pyramidal orchid (*Anacamptis pyramidalis*) and if you are very lucky, the bee orchid (*Ophrys apifera*). **Do not pick the flowers!**

To get there by bus, you must take either the number 130 to Dollymount or the selection of buses which serve Raheny. Only the rare 32X passes the end of the Causeway. Both will add a good half-hour either way onto your walk. There is one advantage: as you walk the Causeway there is plenty of time to observe the waders.

6. Royal Canal —
Leixlip to Maynooth

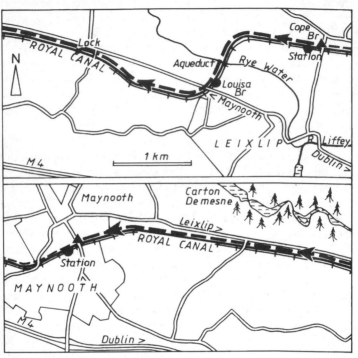

Distance: 8 km
Ascent: Minimal
Time: 2 hours
Equipment: OS Discovery Sheet 50. Trainers (summer), boots (winter).

The Royal Canal is the younger of the two canals that cross Ireland from Dublin to the Shannon. The first, the Grand Canal, was started in 1756 and was finally completed to Shannon Harbour in 1804. The Royal took a more northerly route, was ten miles longer and was only completed to the Shannon at Cloondra, near Tarmonbarry, in 1818. Although it had a few prosperous years, the Royal Canal never carried more than about one-third of the traffic carried by the Grand, and the shareholders were quite glad to sell it to the Midland Great Western

18

Royal Canal — Leixlip to Maynooth

Railway in 1845. The MGWR bought it in order to use the canal bank for its rail line from Dublin to Mullingar, and passenger traffic on the Royal ended. Private traders continued to use the canal to transport peat, agricultural produce (including pigs!), building materials and other bulk items (including Guinness!). However, their numbers declined steadily and after a brief burst of activity during the Second World War, the canal was closed in 1961. Following the closure, low-level road bridges were built across the canal west of Mullingar, and it seemed the Royal was dead, but in recent years there has been a resurgence of interest in canals for recreation. The Royal is now open from Dublin to Mullingar, and work is proceeding on the section to the Shannon, including the removal of the low overbridges.

The towpath from Dublin to Mullingar has been opened as a Waymarked Way, and it is the section of this towpath from Leixlip to Maynooth that I am going to describe. It is easily approached using the suburban rail line from Dublin (Connolly Station) to Mullingar, since the stations are actually beside the canal. Trains operate every two hours except on Sunday. Take the train to Leixlip (Cope Bridge) and return from Maynooth. If you have a car, drive to Maynooth Station, park there beside the Canal, take the train to Leixlip and walk back. Sunday requires the use of the number 66 bus; this adds a good half-hour onto the walk. Or of course you can always use two cars (there's a car park at Leixlip Station). I suggest this as a summer walk when the trees and flowers will be at their best; also, parts of the towpath are rather muddy in winter.

The towpath is on the north side of the Canal, and this first section is dry underfoot, surfaced with chippings. The metal plates every 20 m or so with a number and a fish symbol are for competitions and you may well see a few fishermen here. The rail line is close on the other bank, only swinging away when there is a sharper bend in the canal than the train can take. After twenty minutes or so the canal crosses the Rye Water on an 'aqueduct' — a little disappointing since there are no high masonry arches: it is really a high embankment with a culvert for the stream. Still, it's an impressive view as you peer down at the valley floor and stream many metres below. Building this aqueduct, with the problem of keeping the canal watertight so high above the ground, nearly bankrupted the company. Next is the Louisa Bridge Station and the overbridge of the Leixlip–Maynooth road. When I checked this walk the Way signpost was up on top of the bridge, but the Way actually continues along the towpath under the bridge.

From now on the towpath is unsurfaced and rather muddy, but the whole ambience is more rural with trees on both sides. We met our first swans on this section, standing importantly beside the towpath, quite unmoved as we passed within a metre or so. As you walk, the canal gradually sinks into a cutting with the railway high above, so it is no surprise to reach a hump-back bridge carrying a local road and, immediately beyond, the 13th lock. This is about the halfway mark. Over the next stretch (distinctly muddy in winter) we have rail, water and road transport in close proximity, but fortunately the trees blot out the sight, if not totally the sound, of the passing traffic. The canal is not dead straight so you are spared the frustration of seeing the next bridge until it is only a few minutes away. It carries a road to Celbridge over the canal and railway. The immediate area of the bridge has been tidied up and chipped and there are some seats — a pleasant place to rest and perhaps have a snack.

Now you are on the last lap. The road curves away, the towpath is wide and less muddy, and when the spire of Maynooth church comes in sight you know your destination can't be far off. Soon you reach the new bridge carrying road over rail and canal. Pass under it, and under the old canal bridge and emerge into the Maynooth canal harbour. Recently, this area has been reconstructed and is now most attractive, in great contrast to a photograph I've seen of its decayed condition in 1900. New stonework blends well with old and the wall copings of polished black limestone speckled with white fossils are particularly attractive. When we last visited, a man came to feed the birds. Swans and a few mallard were already on the spot, but more mallard which we had seen a couple of hundred metres further back somehow got the message and came along under the bridges as fast as they could paddle!

Cross the old bridge to the station or your car. The centre of Maynooth is about ten minutes away with pubs and cafés, including one pub with a wonderful mishmash of different interior styles!

Note: The towpath is passable by wheelchair between Cope Bridge and Louisa Bridge and between Maynooth and the bridge on the Celbridge road.

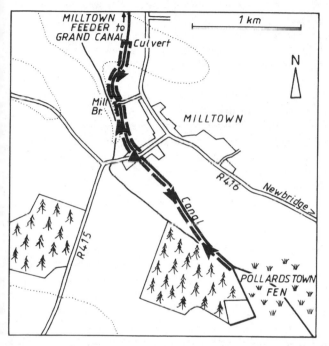

Distance: 3 km south from Milltown Bridge, 2.5 km north
Ascent: Minimal
Time: 1½ hours
Equipment: OS Discovery Sheet 55. Trainers, boots or wellies, depending on time of year and conditions.

Walk 6 took us along a stretch of the Royal Canal. This walk explores a bit of its more successful competitor, the Grand Canal. Luckier than the Royal, the main line of the Grand never closed, though commercial traffic ceased about 1960. It remained open for recreational boats and its future was assured in 1986, when the Inland Waterways Division of the Office of Public Works took over the Grand and other canals. The summit level of the Canal, which is between the 18th and 19th locks near Robertstown, of course requires a steady supply of water to replace that used in locking. Hence the construction of the twelve-kilometre Milltown feeder in the 1780s to supply water from Pollardstown Fen. There's only a few metres' difference in level between the Fen and the Canal, so that the feeder had to be very carefully engineered to get a steady downhill flow, hence the embanked section you will meet on the Walk. It was intended primarily as a feeder, but was also used by barges as far as Milltown, as can be seen from the hump-back bridges and the towpath which runs along its length.

From Dublin take the Naas Road (N7/M7) to the end of the motorway beyond Newbridge, where, after crossing the flyover, you follow the R445 into the middle of Newbridge. At the traffic lights just before the post office turn left onto the R416 which brings you after 5 km to the village of Milltown. Turn left and about 200 m down the road you come to a bridge over the canal; there's a pub here called the Hanged Man's Arch with plenty of room to park beside it. The bridge is a typical high-arched canal bridge, high enough to allow boats to pass underneath.

From the bridge it is possible to walk south on either side of the canal but the west side is easier going. For about 600 m the way is along a wide bank with the canal on the left and fields below on the right. Then the fields give way to rougher, wetter ground, but the bank continues, and soon there is forest on the right. A little further on the feeder splits in two, but the towpath continues along beside the righthand branch. Now you are in Pollardstown Fen. Unusually for Ireland this is a lime-rich bog, fed by springs rising from the edge of the glacial gravels of the Curragh Plains to the south. Here the feeder divides into several branches collecting the water to be channelled down to the Grand Canal. As you go south the land rises imperceptibly until the water in the canal is no longer channelled between dykes above the surrounding country but is lower. This is a bird sanctuary and is also home to a wide variety of plants. On a bright December day, besides the wrens and long-tailed tits bustling among the bushes, a heron took off from its perch, moorhens appeared, and across the canal among the rushes and reeds ducks and waders called continuously.

This unfortunately is a walkers' cul-de-sac, and you must return the same way. For more canal experience continue northward past the bridge, keeping along the west side. Like the southern stretch this can be rather muddy in winter when wellies or waterproof walking boots might be the best footwear. After about a half-kilometre you pass the ivy-clad ruin of an old mill — possibly how the village got its name. You can see traces of the old weir which must have been the outlet for the water from the canal to power the mill.

Almost immediately you come to another hump-back bridge across the canal, but you should continue on the west bank. The surrounding land drops away and the feeder bends around to cross a wide valley on an embankment. At this point, if the water is high, you may have difficulty in crossing a small breach in the canal bank. Assuming the breach is passable, continue along where the path leaves the canal bank and keeps to the foot of the embankment. At the deepest level of the valley a stream runs under the canal in a culvert, with a parallel one for animals, easily passable if one stoops — must be for small cattle! Once on the east side follow the foot of the embankment back to join the towpath on the east bank, and return to the Hangman's.

If the breach isn't passable, it is not far back to the Mill Bridge and you can cross to the east bank and either explore the cattle culvert before returning to the Hangman's or just go straight back there.

The feeder continues north contouring the slope of the Hill of Allen for about 3 km to Pluckerstown Bridge, but there is little of interest and I don't recommend you continue past the culvert.

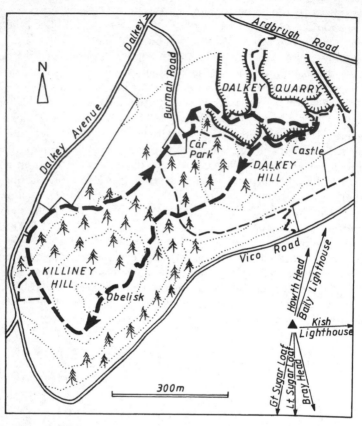

Distance: 2.2 km

Ascent: 220 m

Time: 45 minutes (plus an extra 20 minutes if you start in Dalkey village)

Equipment: OS Discovery Sheet 50 or (better) OS Dublin Street Guide. Trainers, binoculars.

Killiney Hill with Dalkey Quarry is the nearest bit of land to Dublin that could conceivably be called 'wilderness', yet you can savour it and the fine views it offers almost without leaving a surfaced path. On the other hand, if you want to avoid such a path, there are plenty of small tracks through the woods and 'jungle'. It's very popular, of course, and you'll meet walkers, dog exercisers, courting couples, runners and rock-climbers, but you should accept these as part of the entertainment. Nor is it always crowded: when I checked this walk out, on a sunny August Friday evening when the 'tall ships' were coming into Dublin, we met hardly a dozen people.

By car you drive to the car park signposted off Dalkey Avenue which runs up from Dalkey village. If you use public transport, the number 8 bus will take you to the village. Walk up Dalkey Avenue, steep at first and then levelling out, until you see the entrance road to the car park on the left; walk up to the car park itself. This entrance road is locally known as the Burmah Road, but I can't find the origin of this outlandish name!

From the corner of the car park where you enter, follow a path rising through the woods for a few paces before turning left along a vague path across grass which soon enters trees and passes through a wall gap into the Quarry. Don't worry about blasting or mechanical plant — the Quarry was the source of the granite from which Dun Laoghaire Harbour was built in the first half of the last century and it hasn't been worked since. It is now the chief playground for Dublin (and other Irish and even foreign) rock-climbers, and on most summer evenings and weekends all year round you will see them climbing on the cliff above you on the right or in the two bays below you on the left. There are many tracks across the broad level middle area of the Quarry and you can take your pick, provided you keep in view the flight of concrete steps ahead by which you will leave the Quarry. If you head north for 100 m or so along the ridge between the two lower bays, you can see the rope grooves in the trackway where the stones were slid down towards Dun Laoghaire.

When you've had your fill, climb the flight of steps, turn right and climb again to the stone tower overlooking the Quarry. This was originally a telegraph station, and the castellations are purely ornamental. Lean over the wall here to enjoy a superb view over Dublin and Dublin Bay. Below is Dun Laoghaire Harbour, often with a ferry or HSS arriving or a fleet of racing yachts in action.

Beyond are the long sea walls extending into the Bay to form the entrance to Dublin Port, and the low isthmus leading to the Hill of Howth (Walks 3 and 4). As night draws in you can see the flashing beam of the Baily Light on the tip of Howth, and the other beam of the Kish Light on the Kish Bank out to sea.

From the castle continue along the path beside the wall until it begins to drop. Fork left away from the wall and descend, soon with an open wood on your right, to the gap between Dalkey and Killiney Hills. Go straight on at the 'crossroads' and climb Killiney Hill. The path winds upward through the mixed wood of fine trees, many of them with strangely contorted branches. If altitude sickness sets in, you can rest on one of the stone seats beside the path! Soon you emerge onto the open summit of Killiney Hill, with its obelisk, which according to Joyce was probably erected in the exceptionally hard winter of 1741–2 when many fanciful structures were erected to give employment to the poor.

Here is another tremendous view, sweeping right round from Dun Laoghaire and Howth in the north to Dalkey Island and the beaches of Killiney backed by Bray Head (Walk 20), the Little Sugar Loaf (Walk 22), the Great Sugar Loaf (Walk 25) and the Wicklow Mountains in the south. The view was once likened to the Bay of Naples, which presumably accounts for the name Sorrento just below us.

Continue along the path which descends in a wide curve round to the Killiney Hill Road entrance. Here is an imposing gate, a small, square, two-storey, stone gatehouse, built, so the inscription tells us, by Robert Warren in MDCCCLVII, and a modern bronze of Icarus. The path continues, narrower but still surfaced, winding through the woods until it emerges onto open grassland which is crossed to the car park.

Note: A wheelchair can easily reach the obelisk from the Killiney Hill Road gate, and with a little effort by the pusher, from the car park and via that gate. The rest of the circuit unfortunately has too many steps for it to be wheelchair-friendly.

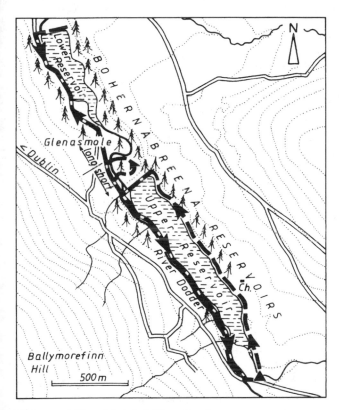

Distance: 3.5 km (short), 5.7 km (long)
Ascent: 25 m (both)
Time: 1 hour (short), 1¾ hours (long)
Equipment: OS Discovery Sheet 50. Trainers.

The Bohernabreena Reservoirs were built in the 1880s to supply water to Rathmines Township, then a separate local authority from Dublin Corporation. Previously the Township obtained its water from the Grand Canal at Gallanstown. This was unsatisfactory and although the Corporation offered water from the Stillorgan Reservoir on the Vartry supply (Walk 31), the Township determined to arrange its own supply. Bickering about this and other matters continued between the two authorities until the Township was absorbed into Dublin in 1930. The walk is of engineering interest because the River Dodder, flowing through the valley, was considered unsuitable because of its high peat content, and it bypasses the Upper Reservoir in a canal. The water in the Upper Reservoir is taken from the peat-free streams to the east, on the side of the Featherbed. The Dodder flows into the Lower Reservoir which is not used for supply, but for flood control. For the curious, the complications of culverts, weirs, channels, spillways, overflow systems, pipes and valves around the reservoirs will offer great possibilities for speculative thinking.

The walk has other attractions. The shores of the reservoirs were planted with pines and larches which have now grown to majestic heights; the shallow upper ends of the two reservoirs have been colonised by reeds and willows, making good bird habitats. The only drawback to all this is that a permit is necessary to enter. This may be obtained very easily (it's free) by phoning the Waterworks Department at 01 679 6111. When you ask for your permit, check the opening hours — they are limited. One phone call is a small price to pay for a fine walk, though it obviously means that you have to plan your visit at least a week or two in advance.

Take the R114 from Dublin through Firhouse. It crosses the Dodder at a right-angle bridge, passes the lower entrance to the Waterworks and continues uphill past a golf club. Take the first turn left, a narrow road which overlooks the reservoirs, and descends to cross the Dodder again just above the Upper Reservoir. Shortly beyond the bridge is a car park on the left, where you stop.

Read all the notices threatening penalties for swimming or polluting the streams, then walk through a kissing gate and take the wide path which follows the shore of the reservoir. This end of the reservoir is attractive with trees and reeds — wonderful reflections on a calm winter day. Soon the path winds between immensely tall and stately pines and larches; sadly many of them are sheathed in masses of ivy, and are so tall their crowns are beginning to droop. Fifteen to twenty minutes brings you to the Upper Dam, which you cross. It is an earth dam, sloping away into woodland. Pause and look up the valley of the Dodder backed by Kippure (757 m), the highest mountain in Co. Dublin, easily recognised by its two television masts. At the far end of the dam you cross the canalised Dodder which drops down beside the dam on a concrete slipway broken by small weirs. You join a narrow tarmac road leading downhill, and shortly you see some granite steps on the right at the top of a path to the valley bottom. Descend the slightly slippery path, turn right and cross a footbridge. You are now between the Dodder and channels from the reservoir — I leave it to you to work out which carries Dublin's water supply. Another path brings you back around to the footbridge. Now there's a choice. There's more to see but it means walking on tarmac beside the Lower Reservoir and coming back the same way.

If you dislike tarmac you will retrace your route back to the top of the dam, and take the path on the west side of the Upper Reservoir, between it and the canalised Dodder. Easy walking, mostly in the open — the fringe of trees is beyond the Dodder. About halfway along there is a curious section where the Dodder is in a tunnel, but every 40–50 m there's a gap about 3 m wide where the river is in the open. After three or four of these openings the tunnel stops and once more the Dodder is in the open. Across the reservoir, on the hillside above the east shore you can see the ruins of a church which was dedicated to St Sentan, a Saxon king's son who came to live in Ireland. Fifteen minutes or so from the Dam brings you past a picnic site (one of several) and a gate onto the road. Turn left and you are at the car park.

If you don't mind a bit of tarmac walking, carry straight on after recrossing the bridge and rejoin the tarmac at the Superintendent's house. Continue along the road beside the west shore of the Lower Reservoir — as I mentioned before, the Dodder flows into this reservoir. Ten minutes brings you to the Lower Dam — a carbon copy of the Upper. The road continues down past the foot of the dam for another 1.3 km to the entrance we passed in the car, but I think you may have had enough tarmac bashing so I recommend you return from here. First take a look over the wall at the spillway below; usually there's a good flow of water and the Dodder curves away out of sight among more magnificent pines and larches. Spare another few minutes to walk across the dam and back and then retrace your steps along the road to the Upper Dam. There join the short route along the west shore of the Upper Reservoir.

10. Three Rock, Fairy Castle and Two Rock Mountains

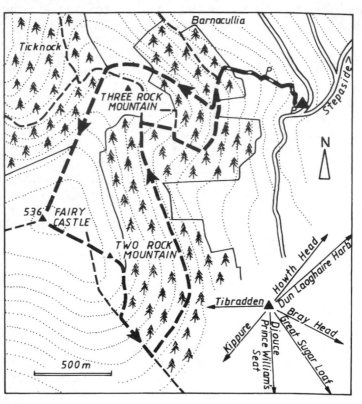

Distance: 6 km

Ascent: 310 m

Time: 2½ hours (allow an extra half-hour if you start from Stepaside)

Equipment: OS Discovery Sheet 50. Boots (trainers possible in summer), stick if you are a little unsteady on rough ground.

Three Rock Mountain (though it might be called Eight Mast Mountain these days) is such an obvious landmark even from the centre of Dublin that it has to be climbed. The only drawback is that so many people have thought so (including those on horseback, on mountain bike and on motorbike) that many of the paths are deeply rutted, and it isn't the place to go on Sunday if you want a bit of solitude. But it's so handy to Dublin, and has such great views, that it mustn't be missed. I've tried to find a route that avoids the crowds as much as possible.

Take the Enniskerry road (R117) to Stepaside and turn right up the road signposted to Glencullen. After about 1 km take a very sharp turn right (it's the second right turn) and in a few metres you will come to a cul-de-sac running uphill. (You can also take the number 44 bus to Stepaside and walk from there.) There's room to park at the entrance to this road or in an open space about 500 m up it. Either way, walk up this road which deteriorates past the last houses into a forest road.

At this point I had better explain that the forest is full of tracks, so many that the OS can't be blamed for not marking them all. My best advice is to stick to the main forest road which bears first left and then right to emerge out of the tree forest onto a stand (if that's the right collective noun!) of masts — and also the eponymous three rocks. They are actually not rocks, but solid outcrops of granite eroded into their present shape by rain and frost. For diversion, they offer easy scrambles. The masts are a horrid eyesore, but I suppose if we must have them for our modern communications, it is best that they should congregate on one hill.

Turn left at the junction and follow the broad track which rises to the south. You are joining the main route from Ticknock and are likely to have company. The track has been badly eroded — it's now a mixture of stones and soft spots — but it rises easily towards Fairy Castle. Before the slope eases, stop and look back: you have perhaps the finest view of Dublin and beyond, on a clear day as far as the Mourne Mountains. When you reach Fairy Castle (536 m) — the remains of a cairn and a trig. point — a new view opens up of the green-brown, rolling Wicklow Mountains to the south and of the Great Sugar Loaf (Walk 25) and Bray (Walk 20) to the east. This is your highest point: the rest is all downhill! I should point out that Three Rock and Two Rock, though both called 'Mountain' on the map, are only shoulders.

Fork left along another clear but rough path past a small outcrop to the Two Rock Mountain, two more upstanding outcrops of granite. Continue to the edge of the trees and follow the rough track down beside the wood. There are several tempting tracks entering the woods, but they will lead you into a criss-cross of unmarked paths which will probably bring you back again (as they did me one day) to the masts. Continue outside the wood, down a steeper section (good views in front of you) until the ground flattens a little and a stile appears. Cross this into the wood and a path leads quickly to a broad, level forest road. It will be quite a relief to get onto good ground underfoot after the rocky, uneven track at the forest edge. Walk this road for about twenty minutes; in the early summer the slight tedium is lightened by the view through the trees of masses of golden gorse below.

When you see a forestry barrier across the road ahead, fork right, then bear right, and finally turn right again at a T-junction. This is less complicated than it sounds, even though the last right turn seems to head you in the wrong direction. It may help your confidence if I add that you are now on a track used for pony trekking and you can probably follow the hoofmarks! The rough track descends steeply, swings round to the left (relief!) and becomes level and easy underfoot. At one point you emerge briefly from the trees, to a good view to Killiney Hill (Walk 8) and — at the right season — a fine show of gorse bloom in the foreground. A few more minutes brings you to your upward route and a short descent to your car, or a longer stroll to Stepaside and good opportunities to rehydrate!

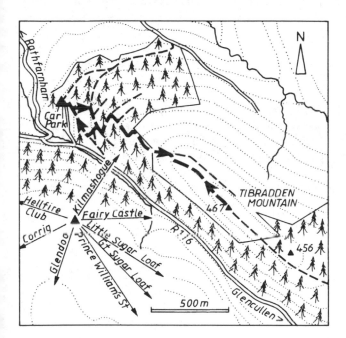

Distance: 3 km
Ascent: 170 m
Time: 1 to 1¼ hours
Equipment: OS Discovery Sheet 50. Boots, weather gear, sticks useful.

This is a short walk for a summer evening or a winter afternoon. Very handy to Dublin, less crowded than the Fairy Castle (Walk 10) and with almost equally good views. It is partly on forest tracks, partly on broad but rough, stony paths. This whole area is known as the Pine Forest, but there has been a lot of felling and what used to be a pleasant walking area across the road to the south is now young trees or felled areas except for a fringe along the road.

Take the R116 out of Dublin, through Rathfarnham and Rockbrook, as it climbs beside the Owendoher River. About 2 km from

Rockbrook the road twists sharply as it crosses a branch of the river; immediately beyond is a T-junction. Turn left and left again into a car park in the forest. Park here. Note that this car park is closed at nightfall, and if you think you are likely to be late returning, park outside the barrier.

It would also be possible to take the number 47A bus to Rockbrook, turn left downhill, cross the bridge, take the road signposted to Larch Hill, turn right after nearly 1 km and continue until the forest and a forest entrance appear on your right. This would add nearly 1½ hours onto the walk time.

At the far end of the car park the tarmac track turns sharply back to form the exit road. A couple of paces along this road, beside a masonry pillar, a grassy track between banks bears left off the tarmac. After about 50 m, a narrow footpath crosses the track. Turn left and climb straight uphill on this path through open, mature woodland to a forest road contouring the slope. Unfortunately from here on, until you hit the heather hillside, you are among young trees.

Turn right and follow the road past a branch on the left and a footpath on the right with a painted arrow pointing downhill. The road swings uphill to the left and deteriorates (rainwater has created gullies). At the next junction turn right and follow the increasingly gullied track which turns sharply left at an old timber barrier and climbs to the edge of the wood. This all sounds very complicated, but I think it is fairly simple to follow on the ground. If in trouble, follow paths that lead UP; the old timber barrier is a good landmark.

Now the track, increasingly stony, climbs between the young forest and a fence, before leaving the forest and hugging the fence as it climbs between banks of deep heather. Quite soon the main track swings away from the fence and keeps to the crest of the rounded ridge leading to the summit. The angle eases and the summit comes into view; all that is left is to negotiate the rather rough track to the summit (467 m) with its cairn and round chamber. Joyce says that on the south side of one of the summit rocks there's 'a rude carving of a cross and human face', which he opines is at least one hundred years old. I haven't found it, but there is an inscribed stone in the cairn. Last time I was up there the wind was so strong that I was glad to be inside the chamber, able to peer over the top at the view, ducking when the wind got too strong, like a lookout in a trench dodging shells. (But I have also picnicked up there on a sunny summer evening without a breath of wind — such are the vagaries of weather on even such a small hill as this one.)

The view? Going clockwise from the rounded, heathery dome of Fairy Castle directly to the east, there are the Little Sugar Loaf (Walk 22) — two summits from this angle — and the Great Sugar Loaf (Walk 25) both peeping over the nearer hills, Prince William's Seat (Walk 16) and Glendoo to the south, Corrig Mountain far away to the south-west. Dublin Port is hidden behind Fairy Castle, but the west part of the city is visible between the Hellfire Club (Walk 12) to the west and nearby Kilmashogue to the north.

The return is by the same route, except that I suggest you turn down into the mature woodland on the arrowed path I mentioned on the way up. Where this path swings away to the left, keep straight on to meet the grassy track you started on and follow it back to the car park. I suggest this because it's easier to find than the top end of the path you climbed up.

You are so near Dublin that you may want to go straight into town, but there is a pleasant little pub on the righthand side of the road below Rockbrook as you return to Rathfarnham.

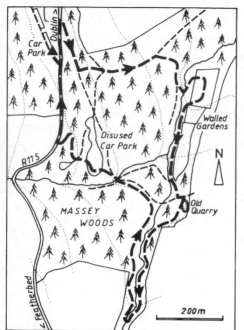

Distance:
Massey Woods 3 km
Hellfire Club 2 km

Ascent:
Massey Woods 170 m
Hellfire Club 240 m

Time:
Massey Woods 1 hour
Hellfire Club ¾ to 1 hour

Equipment:
OS Discovery Sheet 50
Trainers.

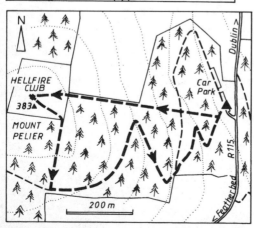

The 'Hellfire Club' on the summit of Mount Pelier is a landmark visible from many parts of Dublin. What is much less visible but actually more attractive for walking are the woods below the road to the Featherbed. It is Coillte, the Irish Forestry Board, property but there is very little modern conifer planting. Instead we find a wonderful variety: open wood of beech and oak, a rhododendron jungle fringing the stream, and magnificent pines, 50 m or so in height. The tracks in the Massey Woods are much more complicated than are shown on the OS map, so I've made the sketch map more detailed, and also the instructions. If you do get lost, go uphill — you'll hit the road somewhere! There's only one danger in these woods — daredevil mountain bikers!

Take the R115 out from Rathfarnham. It climbs steeply up beside Mount Pelier, and about 5.5 km from Rathfarnham you pull into the car park on the right of the road. Note: this car park is closed at night — check the closing time and if in doubt, there is some parking space outside the gate.

First the Massey Woods. Go back to the road, and walk back towards Dublin for 120 m to the forest entrance below the road. Go down the forest road for about 150 m and turn off left onto a rather vague path leading down to a Y-junction. You are heading into the 'V' of the 'Y' so you can hardly go wrong. Carry on down the stem of the 'Y' through open, mature wood. When you reach open ground on the left, turn right onto a path which winds down to the stream and crosses it. This stream and its surroundings are the best part of the walk. Once across, turn left, cross another stream and almost immediately go through an arch in the high wall into a decayed garden enclosure. Turn right, passing the remains of two ornamental ponds, and after climbing two short sets of steps and reaching a cross wall, turn right again out of the garden onto a path above the stream. Just here is an open glade with a group of huge, tall, straight pine trees.

The path winds among rhododendrons with the wall on one side and the stream gurgling and splashing over rocks below. Here and there you pass a small ruin; or set of steps leading nowhere — intriguing sources of curiosity as to their origin and use (one was an ice-house). Along here too are many large mature trees. The wall ends and the path meets a road. Quick turns left and right bring you up to a disused quarry and a path which once more overlooks the rocky stream. If you've had enough, you can cross at a small bridge about 150 m further on, but I prefer to follow the winding path further up the stream. You begin to climb, the stream pours down small cascades, and the wooded valley narrows with open fields on either side. You emerge suddenly from the rhododendrons and there's a bridge. Cross it and walk down the other side of the stream. The OS map marks a 'megalithic tomb' hereabouts. It's a small, unexciting heap of stones between two gullies, not really worth the effort of climbing up to! Soon you pass the short-cut bridge and then meet the road, which you follow to the left to a big bridge. Across the bridge a path on the left will take you uphill past the end of a parking area (closed at present) and on up to the road. Turn right along the road, and you are soon back to your starting point.

Now for the Hellfire Club. This area is mostly recent plantings of conifers and does not bear comparison with the Massey Woods, but the Hellfire Club definitely merits a visit. 'Hellfire Club' is a misnomer. It was built in 1725 as a summer residence by William Conolly of Castletown House, Speaker of the Irish House of Commons, and although the Hellfire Club may perhaps have met there occasionally, it was not their regular meeting place.

Near the south (entrance) end of the car park a track diagonals through the wood, leading almost at once to a wider path running straight up the hill (I am taking you up the steep way and down the easy way — I think this suits most people). The path crosses a forest road and continues straight up. After a bit, open ground appears on the right, and higher up you emerge onto a big square of open grass with the Hellfire Club in the middle. It's an impressive building! The first slated roof blew off because, it is said, of the sacrilegious act of the builder in using the stones from the nearby megalithic tomb. Speaker Conolly then built the existing corbelled stone roof, an almost unique feature. As late as Weston Joyce's visit about 1912, there were dramatic views all round; now only the view to the north over the city remains, but it is fine indeed, especially if you are up there as evening draws in and the lights come on.

Walk across the grass to the south-east corner of the open ground and pick up a path leading through the wood and out to a good forest road. Turn left along this road which zigzags down the hill. Just beyond the second bend a path drops off to the right and leads you back down to the car park.

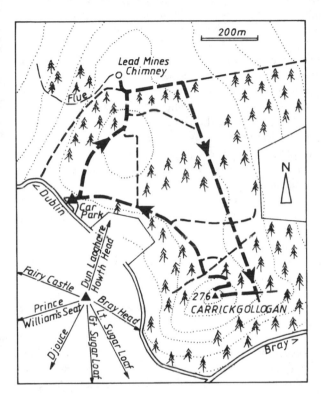

Distance: 2 km
Ascent: 90 m
Time: ¾ hour
Equipment: OS Discovery Sheet 50 for the walk, but bring Sheet 56 for the view to the south. Runners OK, but boots (rubber or walking) are a good idea after rain — people, horses and mountain bikes have made the tracks muddy in places.

If you follow the Enniskerry road (R117) through Stepaside you will see ahead and slightly to your left a tall chimney, the Lead Mines chimney, and to its right a rounded hilltop rising above the trees. The hill — at 276 m we can hardly call it a mountain — is Carrickgollogan, better known to Dubliners as 'Kattygollogher'. Together with the chimney, it makes a pleasant and popular walk on a summer evening or winter afternoon. I expect dawn would be good too, but I've never tried that!

Follow the R117 from Dundrum and 0.4 km beyond Kilternan, opposite a terrace of houses, take a narrow road on the left. This road will lead you in about 2 km to a ridge top and a left turn. Follow this as it bends round to the right and turn left into the car park (closed at time of writing, but there is room to park on the road).

Take the track towards the forestry ahead and beyond the barred gate leave the track for a narrow path on the left which meanders diagonally up an open slope of gorse and undergrowth to a fringe of very battered and burnt trees — there was a catastrophic fire here some years ago. The path goes on beside the trees to meet a forest track onto which you turn left into woodland. In a couple of minutes you emerge and there is the chimney directly ahead. A muddy path leads to its base. It is a tapering tower built of large granite blocks; a stairway of stone treads spirals up it snake-like, with a few of the lower treads removed to discourage adventurers. A 1900 photograph in Joyce shows that it has lost quite a lot of height since then.

A little to the left among the gorse bushes you can find the remains of the tunnel (flue) which connected the old lead smelting works below at Ballycorus to the chimney. Lead was mined there in the nineteenth century; this ore, together with the ore brought by cart from Glendalough, was smelted in Ballycorus, and the resultant gases taken away up the flue to the chimney. The lead sulphate in the gases condensed on the masonry of the flue while the remaining gases were taken up through the chimney into the atmosphere. Every few months the smelting would stop, and when the flue had cooled and the air cleared, workers would go in and scrape the lead off the flue walls. Not unexpectedly there was a high mortality among the workers from lead poisoning. Spend a few minutes here, to explore the flue (from outside!) and to admire the magnificent mature Scots pines further down the hill.

Return to the edge of the wood and turn left along the broad track beside it. It descends gently and very soon you will find a junction to the right which you follow under a line of electric pylons. To your right are young trees, to your left beyond an old overgrown wall the scattered remains of sad, old trees left by the fire. Carrickgollogan is straight ahead, a dark curve against the sky on a winter's afternoon with, as I last saw it, two small silhouetted figures on the top, looking as high and as far off as Mont Blanc.

Don't worry, it is only a few minutes away. The forest road is crossed by another and deteriorates into a wide, rough path between young trees as it climbs to a saddle. There, beside a pylon, turn right up a path through woodland, finely carpeted with needles. After a few metres you emerge onto the slope of Carrickgollogan which you climb by any one of several narrow, braided paths which wind up steeply among heather and white quartzite scree. The summit (276 m) is reached in an easy but satisfying half-hour from the car park.

The flat open summit offers great views all round. To the north and east is Dun Laoghaire and Dalkey (Walk 8) and the spread of Dublin Bay, with almost always a ship or two approaching or leaving the Port. Turn south to see Bray Head (Walk 20) and the successively higher quartzite summits of the Little (Walk 22) and the Great (Walk 25) Sugar Loaf. Further round again as you sweep from south-west to north-west are the Wicklow Mountains from Djouce to Fairy Castle (Walk 10).

For the descent, face towards the car park and you will find a rough but easy-angled zigzag path back into the trees and to a forest road which will lead you straight back to the car park. (You can of course reverse this walk, but I think most people prefer a steep ascent to a steep descent, and the Carrickgollogan summit makes a good climax.)

Note: Although the route suggested is unsuitable for a wheelchair, the main forest tracks are reasonably flat and well surfaced.

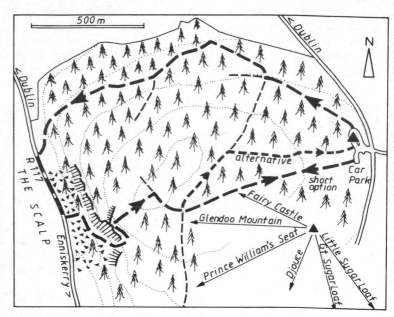

Distance: 2 km (long), 1.2 km (short)
Ascent: 100 m (long), 30 m (short)
Time: 1 hour (long), ½ hour (short)
Equipment: OS Discovery Sheet 50. Boots or non-slip trainers, sticks useful (long), trainers (short).

The 'long' walk is an 'Adventure Walk', not for the faint-hearted or those at all unsteady on their legs. It is an exploration of the Scalp, that deep gash in the hills of County Dublin through which the road goes to Enniskerry. There is only a miserable little stream in it now, obviously quite incapable of having carved its way 100 m down through solid granite. It is in fact a glacial overflow channel, cut at the end of the Ice Age when the melting ice created a great lake of melt water trapped between the ice to the north and the Dublin Mountains. Eventually the water rose high enough to top the ridge and the power of the huge volume of escaping water cut out the Scalp as we know it. Even to drive through it, with steep rocky slopes on either side, is dramatic enough; but to fully appreciate it needs some output of pedestrian energy. I don't want older or less fit walkers to feel deprived, so I have included a shorter and much easier variant.

Take the Enniskerry road (R117) out of Dublin and 0.4 km beyond Kilternan, opposite a terrace of houses, take a narrow road on the left. This road will lead you in about 2 km to a crest and a junction to the left (the way to Walk 13). Immediately opposite is the entrance to Barnaslingan car park (closed at time of writing, but it is possible to park on the road).

At the north end of the car park, to the east of the electricity pylon, an unobtrusive gap in the wire fence takes you onto a good path, at first through scrub, and then through the mainly conifer mature forest which is a feature of the Scalp. After a few minutes a steep, narrow path drops down from the left and continues downhill on your right. Follow it down. Soon it levels out and curves left, sometimes hard to follow where the ground underfoot is a carpet of pine needles. However, if you follow the line of least resistance you will soon locate the path again which debouches onto a broad forest track at a sharp bend. Turn right and a few more minutes will bring you to a timber gate onto the road through the Scalp.

Turn left along the road, which unfortunately is extremely busy. The pavement soon peters out but there is a verge, and anyway it is only 150 m to a gate where the old road went straight on and the new road swerves right. Beside the gate the wall has collapsed. Scramble through it (I am sorry to say there is quite a lot of cans and plastic). You are now going to climb up the side of the Scalp and though it is quite rough going it is not as bad as it looks, though sometimes you will find your hands useful. There are other possibilities than the way I describe, but **be careful; it is very easy to climb up, but much harder to descend if you've made a mistake.**

Go up a couple of metres left and you will find a faint path which winds up among the trees and rocks. However, it is better to rely on your eyes and intelligence than to look for the 'path'. Bear a little right towards the foot of a massive slab of rock; keep below a pointed boulder below the slab; then climb gently leftward, below the main rocky walls and above the scree. This leads you across towards a rib of rock which continues down below your level. On the near side of it a wide, steep, grassy slope brings you up to easy ground above the rocks.

Turn left onto a vague path which keeps along the top of the cliffs, rising to the highest point where you will find a wonderful belvedere. Almost sheer below, the puny little cars crawl along the road; opposite, the rocky west wall of the Scalp is crowned with trees; beyond is a panorama of mountains, ranging from the Little Sugar Loaf (Walk 22) to the left, past its Great brother (Walk 25), past Djouce and Maulin (Walk 23), past Prince William's Seat (Walk 16) to Fairy Castle (Walk 10). On a winter afternoon, they form a hard-edged, dark silhouette, as though cut by a knife.

Turn reluctantly away and now, faced with a variety of small paths, try to walk as near as you can at right angles to the line of cliffs — I can't be more specific, there are too many of them! You climb a little and then descend gently on a needle carpet, and ahead you will be able to pick out a forest road. You should hit the road at or near a T-junction. Take the vertical of the T and a few minutes will bring you back, past a forest barrier, to the car park.

The short route reverses the return of the long route, taking the main forest road to the T, and going straight ahead through the wood and across the open hilltop to the cliff edge. After suitable viewing time return to the T, and either retrace your outward way, or, if you want a little variety, turn left along the forest track, and take the next good path to the right which will bring you straight back to the car park.

Whichever route you pick, take time to wander among the trees; unlike so many of our forests, grown for commercial timber, these trees are here for you to enjoy, and it is a pleasure to walk among them on the soft floor of pine needles.

The number 44 bus to Enniskerry goes through the Scalp quite frequently and will drop you at its Dublin end. Walk along and either turn in at the wooden gate and reverse the outward long route to reach the car park, or continue along the road to pick up the scrambling ascent. All sorts of combinations possible!

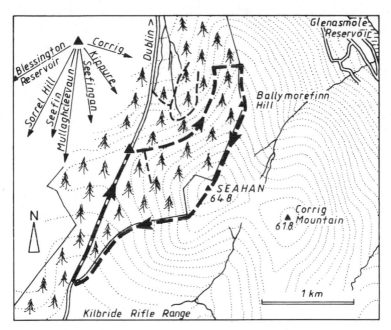

Distance: 6.5 km
Ascent: 300 m
Time: 2½ hours
Equipment: OS Sheets 50 and 56 — it's just on the edge of both. Boots, weather gear, stick useful, compass if the weather is doubtful.

In Scotland all the mountains above 3,000 ft are called 'Munros' after the first man to climb them all, Sir Hugh Munro. The Irish equivalent are the 2,000 ft mountains (now modified to 600 m) and sometimes called 'Vandeleurs' after one of the makers of the first list. Seahan is the nearest to Dublin and so deserves our interest. It also has both a round barrow and a cairn on its summit. The walk is almost all on paths, but they are rough and boggy in places, hence my recommendation of boots and a stick. The only drawback to this walk is the final half-hour along a road.

Take the R114 out of Dublin, through Rathfarnham and Old Bawn, past the entrance to the Bohernabreena Waterworks and up to the top of the hill beyond. There take a turn left signposted Kilbride, drive for about 2.7 km and park at the second forest entrance on the left (just on the bottom edge of Sheet 50). Take the forest road past the barrier. Hardly rising, it makes a wide sweep around to the north among mature trees, on a side slope steep enough to allow views of the Swift Brook valley below. After twenty minutes or so it comes to an abrupt end, but a steep, rocky path goes straight up the hill and emerges onto the open heathery hillside of the long ridge between Ballymorefinn Hill and Slievenabawnoge. There is a good track just inside the forest fence — go left along it.

I came across an extract about a Mass Rock around here. It was vague about its location, but an old man I met told me it was near the top of the steep path. Visible on the heather slope a short distance above the forest fence is a pile of granite boulders. I think this must be the Mass Rock: it looks like the rough sketch in the extract, and fulfils the criteria in the extract that it could be approached from the Swift Brook or from the Corrig Brook which runs down the other side of the ridge. I should explain for foreign visitors that in the seventeenth and eighteenth centuries the celebration of Mass was forbidden and Catholic priests could be executed if caught, so that Mass used to be said secretly high up in the hills.

Now at last we have turned south and are heading towards Seahan! It is still invisible; the heather-covered hill you see ahead and a bit to the left is Corrig Mountain. Soon you breast the rise and Seahan appears ahead with the track heading straight to it. The flat ground brings its inevitable Wicklow concomitant, morass, and you may find it expedient to cross the decrepit wire fence and take to the slightly drier path on the other side, returning once the track starts climbing again. Seahan now looks close but I have to warn you that it has two deceptive false summits before the trig. pillar (648 m) finally comes into sight, perched on top of a prehistoric stone cairn. Incidentally, Sheet 56 shows the whole summit area as forested — this is an error. Just before you reach it you pass some long stone slabs on edge; follow them round, they are the stones which edge a round barrow, a Newgrange in miniature. Climb onto it and you can see the remains of the tomb chamber. As far as I know this has never been excavated and isn't dated. You will have a fine view of the Dublin Mountains, from nearby Corrig, swinging south to Kippure, spoilt by its television masts, to Seefingan and Seefin, each with a chamber tomb of its own.

Behind Seefin you can see Mullaghcleevaun (Walk 30) and Sorrel Hill (Walk 24) and out to the south-west and west the Blessington Reservoirs and the Central Plain. You are standing just about in the centre of the half-circle which the River Liffey makes, from its source beyond Kippure, into the reservoir and out to the west before swinging north and then east to Dublin and the sea.

Corrig blocks the view to the east; it can be included in the walk, though it will add about forty-five minutes and take you well over my self-imposed three-hour limit. Just head straight for it, picking handy sheep tracks if you can; the heather does not make easy walking. From the summit (618 m) you look down on the upper Dodder valley and the Bohernabreena Reservoirs (Walk 9) and across to the Hellfire Club (Walk 12). On the return, no need to reclimb Scahan, just contour round to the south.

From Seahan walk a few metres south to the steel tubular post which marks the boundary of the Kilbride Rifle Range. From the post, the corner of the forest is easily seen; walk down the heather to reach it. (I include a compass in the equipment list in case the summit is in cloud; go south-west and you'll find the wood without difficulty.) A broad, rough track leads down, steeply at first, beside the wood and then the slope eases. Occasionally you will see a Range marking pole on your left and there are also some carved granite pillars of an earlier era, on which you can read with difficulty that the actual boundary is in the middle of the stream on your right.

At this stage you become annoyingly aware that the forest edge is swinging you away from your car. The OS Sheet shows some tempting paths in the forest, but I have been unable to find them; they don't reach the forest edge. Nothing for it but to continue down the track, which is rather rough and occasionally wet, until you can cross a fence and a gully to reach the road (passing a board which disclaims any responsibility for anything that might happen to you on the Rifle Range — don't worry, the track you have come down is used regularly by walkers without accident).

Turn right and walk the road (sorry!) back to the start.

Seahan

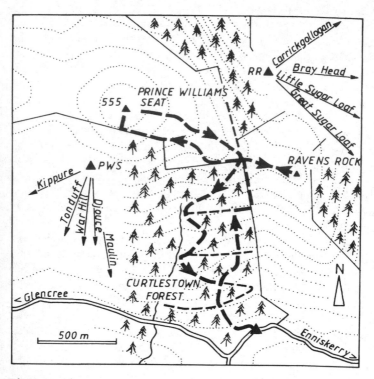

Distance: 6 km
Ascent: 300 m
Time: 2¼ to 2½ hours
Equipment: OS Discovery Sheet 56. Boots (trainers possible in summer), weather gear, compass if the weather is doubtful.

This is a pleasant afternoon or summer evening walk with plenty of variety. It is all on forest roads or paths — partly on the Wicklow Way (which is the only track marked on the OS map). At time of writing there are beautiful stands of tall, well-spaced fir trees in the lower forest, but I cannot promise that Coillte, the Irish Forestry Board, won't fell them. The open part of the walk is through deep heather which is why

48

I've kept to paths on the hill, although they are mostly fairly rough! You may wonder a little at the complexity of the walk: that's because I've designed it so that you retrace your steps as little as possible! The views, as so often from middle-height outliers, are good.

Take the Glencree road out of Enniskerry for 4 km to the Curtlestown Forest entrance (P on the OS map) where you leave your car. Follow the forest road among the fir trees I have mentioned until you come to a sharp turn right — there is a Wicklow Way (Yellow Man) marker there. Just beyond the marker take to a narrow footpath going more or less straight up the hill (young trees on your right). You cross the road zigzagging back and continue along the footpath which meanders pleasantly uphill to another forest road. Many old walls and a few ruins testify that this was once farmland. Cross the road and climb straight up — more steeply and without benefit of a good path — towards the light at the top of this dark wood to reach yet another forest road. Turn right and follow it out of the wood.

The rocks you see in front are, unfortunately, not Ravens Rock, so turn left and climb a narrow, twisty path beside the wood. Soon the real Ravens Rock comes in sight, and you can either head directly for it — but it's rough going! — or continue up to the corner of the forest and pick up another path which leads to the rocks.

Fine views reward you — from the Great Sugar Loaf (Walk 25) on the right, over the Little Sugar Loaf (Walk 22) — very dull from this direction, Bray Head (Walk 20) and Bray with the Irish Sea behind, to Carrickgollogan (Walk 13) and the Scalp (Walk 14) with Dublin in the haze beyond. If you want to picnic, there is an excellent little patch of grass well sheltered by big rocks on the west side of the summit.

Now you must retrace your steps to the corner of the wood where you will find a Yellow Man marker. There are two paths up to Prince William's Seat (I haven't found the origin of the name), and I take you up one and down the other, mainly because it is hard to find the point where the straighter one leaves the Wicklow Way. So cross the Way and follow the broad track beside the wood for 100 m or so, turn right and keep along the track (boggy in places I'm afraid) which curves round to meet the forest fence again and climbs comfortably to the shoulder of Prince William's Seat. Where the track levels out, leave it and climb easily (soft and dry underfoot after heather burning) towards the trig. pillar of the Seat, which is almost immediately visible. From the summit (555 m) there are good views west and south of the Wicklow Mountains, from Kippure with its television masts on the right to Tonduff and Maulin (Walk 23) with War Hill and Djouce behind. The swell of the hill hides some of the view you had from Ravens Rock.

Two not very obvious paths lead back — the right hand is the one you want. It's a bit vague, and while obvious enough on a fine day, a compass would be helpful in mist. It will bring you back to the Wicklow Way, on open ground some 50 m before the top of the forest. All you have to do now is follow the Way back to the start. It's a rough path between the rocks and trees to begin with but after a few minutes it turns into a good forest road which takes you down easily and swiftly in wide zigzags to rejoin your outward route in the open forest.

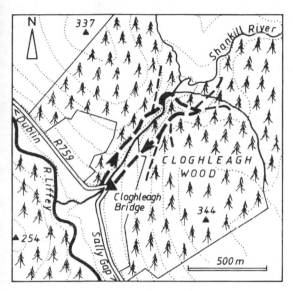

17. Cloghleagh Wood

Distance: 2 km
Ascent: 70 m
Time: ¾ hour
Equipment: OS Discovery Sheet 56. Trainers.

This is a short, easy, pleasant, woodland walk, much of it beside a stream, with views of the upper Liffey valley as it flows down from its source on the slopes of Tonduff. It is perhaps hardly worth a special visit, but is a very good leg-stretcher for anyone visiting the Upper Liffey by car. If you have reached Cloghleagh by the suggested route from Dublin, you have two equally recommendable return routes by motor. One continues up the Liffey to the Sally Gap, turns left onto the Military Road which contours round the boggy hillside, past Liffey Head, Upper Lough Bray (Walk 19) and the Featherbed to Dublin. The other turns off the R759 at Ballysmuttan Bridge (a busy picnic spot on summer Sundays), climbs to the Ballynultagh Gap below Sorrel Hill (Walk 24) and drops down — fine views over Pollaphuca Reservoir — to Blessington and the N81.

Take the N81 Blessington road out of Dublin. Three kilometres past Brittas village (the Blue Gardenia pub) turn left on the R759, signposted Kilbride. After 1.5 km the R759 goes sharply left at a junction (follow the sign for Sally Gap — watch you don't go straight on!). The road crosses a bridge, swings sharp right almost immediately, and carries on past Mooney's pub on the right. You are now heading east towards the mountains up the valley of the young River Liffey which winds its way on the right towards Pollaphuca Reservoir. Continue for 3 km (4.5 km from the N81). The road enters a forest, and at a sharp righthand bend crosses a stream. There are stone walls on each side and the bridge has a low balustrade of granite pillars. There is room to park carefully on the left here — please do not obstruct the road.

The stream is the Shankill River, a tributary of the Liffey. Here it is dropping steeply down over granite steps in a very attractive small gorge under young beech forest. A place to linger, or for a pleasant brief stroll go down the right (west) bank towards the Liffey through open oak and beech forest. For a longer walk go back (west) for 100 m from the bridge to a forest track with a barrier on the right. Take this track which climbs up the valley above the river, with spruce plantations to the left and beech woods running steeply down to the river below on the right. The track climbs higher and higher above the river, passing a magnificent old fir tree on the far bank. Then the trees on the far bank give way to rhododendrons, the valley opens out, the river bed becomes flatter and gravelly, and you come to a bridge, just below the confluence of two tributaries.

Before you, in the open valley, the main stream can be seen winding its way down between low hills. There is scope for more exploration along the streams from here and further along the walk. But do not behave like some of the users of the area who leave their rubbish!

Stay on the track across the bridge and up the hill away from the main stream, past a junction to the left, now with pine forest on the right and open land on the left. Soon you come to a second junction — turn right to face a short, sharp climb among dark young sitka spruce trees to the high point of the walk. As you leave the spruce and come into the open pines you can hear the river again, now far below. The main track veers left up into the forest, but ignore this and keep right along a level grassy track. After about 400 m a fence crosses the track where it leaves the forest, and straight ahead Sorrel Hill (Walk 24) looks imposing. About 30 m before the fence find a small path which veers off to the right. It runs diagonally down the slope at a fairly gentle angle between two old overgrown stone walls, the remains of an old roadway. Spruce on the left gives way first to pine trees and then to oaks and as the path levels out you return to a young beech wood. Straight ahead a stile provides a way across the fence back to the main road.

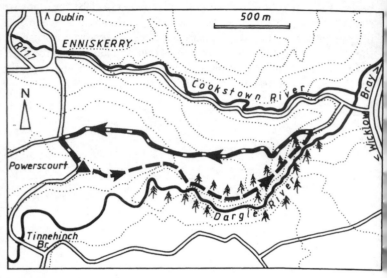

Distance: 3.5 km
Ascent: 90 m
Time: 1 hour (1½ hours starting from Enniskerry)
Equipment: OS Discovery Sheet 56. Trainers (gumboots in winter). *No fishing rods!*

It so happens that the weather has been less than perfect whenever I've done this walk. Once, snow was lying low on the hills and there were wonderful views over the bare trees to the Great Sugar Loaf (Walk 25). When I checked the route for this guide it was a damp day in May with an unbroken pale grey sky. The Sugar Loaf had disappeared behind the grey curtain; Carrigoona (Walk 21) looked really big; and a thin film of mist muffled the outlines of the woods across the Dargle. A great experience both times!

Take the Enniskerry road (R117) out of Dublin, go through Enniskerry to the top of the hill. The road bears left at the

Powerscourt entrance; park on the wide verge just before the road swings sharply right again towards Tinnehinch Bridge. Exactly on the corner a narrow laneway heads east. If using public transport, take the quite frequent number 44 bus to Enniskerry and walk up the hill. This will add ten to fifteen minutes each way to your time.

Follow the laneway which quickly narrows to a footpath between overgrown fences. To your right the deep valley of the River Dargle lies beyond a field, with woods rising beyond. From the numerous gaps you can pick out the views I've mentioned. You pass through the battered remains of an old sheet-iron gate and continue, now with woods on your left. This stretch has puddles after rain — hence my suggestion of gumboots! You pass a ruin that sprouts ivy from the tops of its walls and then the path enters the woods which clothe the Dargle gorge. It's an old mixed forest: oak, ash, conifers, shrubs and intruding rhododendron. You can hear the river below, and there are several very steep little paths leading down to it. They are fun to explore, and the river in its gorge is a great attraction, but they are slippery, and there is one easy access further down. On one of these pathlets you see a notice saying 'Dargle Anglers' Club — Members Only'; this refers to fishing and explains that ban on fishing rods in 'Equipment'.

Watch out after about twenty minutes for a bare outcrop of rock on your right; walk to its prow for a tremendous, plunging view over the gorge. Continue down the path, now more open with occasional viewpoints. Another five or ten minutes brings you to a fairly level path on your right. This leads to the river in a couple of minutes and it is worth the diversion to see the brown, boggy water foaming over rapids and a high, dripping crag overhanging the far bank — a scene that looks as if it came straight from a nineteenth-century print. But don't disturb the anglers — they have priority here and won't appreciate a noisy group! A few more minutes along the path, now wider and flatter, brings you through a gate onto a road.

You can return to your car or to Enniskerry by retracing your steps or by turning left up the road. It is rather narrow and twisty, but not too busy, and after a bit there is a footpath on the right side screened from the road by a hedge. You meet the main road opposite Powerscourt entrance. Turn left for your car or right for Enniskerry where you can easily find refreshments for all tastes.

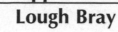
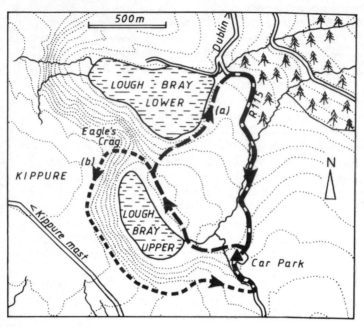

Distance: 3 km (short), 3.3 km (long)
Ascent: 110 m (short), 130 m (long)
Time: 1 hour (short), 1½ hours (long)
Equipment: (Both) OS Discovery Sheet 56. Boots, sticks useful (long only), weather gear, compass if weather is doubtful.

Many Dubliners driving over the Featherbed and along the Military Road will have noticed on the right the dark lake in the valley below the frowning scarp of the upper slopes of Kippure. To connect the two Loughs makes an easy walk in a fine landscape, but beware: it is boggy and the path, through much use, alternates between soft depressions and protruding rocks. Hence the suggestion of sticks if you are no longer young (or middle-aged) and agile.

Take the R115 out of Dublin past the Hellfire Club car park (Walk 12) and continue over the bare Featherbed where you will often see people still 'winning' the turf by hand. The road swoops down to the head of Glencree passing in the woods on the left Glencree House, which started life as a Barracks. It was one of a series along the 'Military Road' which was driven right through the centre of the Wicklow Mountains to Glendalough, Glenmalure and Aughrim to flush out the 'rebels' who had taken refuge there after the failure of the 1798 Rebellion. It became a Reformatory for young offenders, then a place of internment for German aviators during the Second World War (officially 'The Emergency'), and lastly a Reconciliation Centre which has done much good work promoting peace in Northern Ireland. Ignoring two left junctions, continue along the Military Road, which passes a cottage which used to dispense tea (but is now boarded up) and then climbs in sweeping bends towards Kippure. Stop in the parking area of an abandoned quarry; the path starts immediately on the opposite (low) side of the road.

The path, rough, irregular, occasionally boggy but always well defined, descends to Upper Lough Bray, crossing the outlet. Two paths skirt the north-east shore; one scrambles along close to the water line, the other — preferable I think — takes the crest of a low, heathery ridge. This can be an awesome place when dark clouds threaten from the west: the scarp of Kippure is gloomy, the Lough almost black. But let the sun come out and all is changed! At the far end of the Lough, on the ridge which divides the Upper from the Lower Lough, the path forks and you must make a choice. Either continue down beside the Lower Lough or bear left and climb the imposing rocky nose, the Eagle's Crag, towards Kippure.

Let us take the easy route first ((a) on the sketch map). The path winds down beside the Lower Lough, more open than its namesake, with a fine house surrounded by trees (private land unfortunately) on the far shore. All this area along with Glencree, Joyce tells us, was a royal forest in the Middle Ages. There was plenty of deer poaching; even the Abbot of St Mary's Abbey in Dublin which owned property nearby was caught poaching in 1291. Later the government of the Pale was glad to cut down the trees — they were 'the seat and nursery of rebellion'. It won't take you long to reach the road beside the cottage. Then, I'm afraid, you have to follow the road back to your starting point. It is busy on Sunday afternoon, but fairly quiet at other times.

The more exciting route ((b) on the sketch map) takes you along the crest of the ridge between the Loughs with the Lower Lough spread out below you. Then you climb the nose. It looks difficult but a steep little zigzag path, invisible from a distance, will take you up quite easily, though you may like to pull on the heather now and again to help you over an even steeper step. It brings you to the top of the scarp beside the rocky granite nose from where, across heather and bog, you can see the two television masts on Kippure summit. Turn left and find the irregular muddy track which keeps near the edge of the scarp. On a clear day, following this track is not difficult; but in mist a compass is useful further on where the track leaves the scarp edge, becomes less distinct and breaks up into branches each searching for the driest route. Soon you will see the electrical poles leading to the television masts with the road beyond. Aim just left of the one nearest the road, cross the nascent Glencree stream, and scramble up to the road, which you reach less than 100 m from the car park. Either return to Dublin by the same route or turn off down Glencree and follow a winding road to Enniskerry, with a wide selection of pubs and cafés.

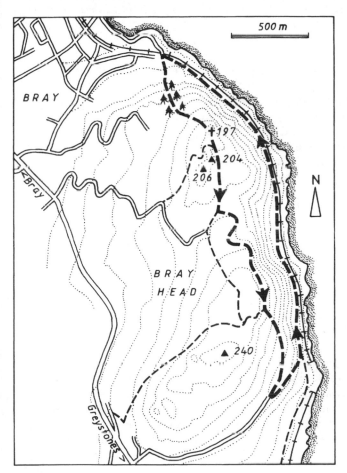

Distance: (from car park) 6 km
Ascent: 210 m
Time: 2¼ hours (allow an extra half-hour from the DART station)
Equipment: OS Discovery Sheet 56. Trainers; sticks useful.

Bray Head

Bray Head offers a delightful, varied walk. A quite steep climb to a viewpoint, a high-level ridge walk, and a return along a cliff path above rocky coves, small promontories, and on a windy day magnificent waves battering the rocks. Add to all this the fact that the walk is accessible by bus or by suburban train — and what more could you desire in two hours?

Assuming that you have a car, you should park at the southern end of the Promenade, or if there is no space, take the exit under the railway, turn left, left again to another car park. The number 45 bus will leave you at the southern end of the Promenade, the DART about a kilometre further back.

From the Promenade you can see a big cross high up on a rocky summit — that's where you are heading! Follow the broad, concrete path which winds up from the end of the Front; cross the railway and a short distance beyond at a sharp bend there is a branch up the hill to the right, complete with a safety railing just like those outside school entrances. (The path from the upper car park joins just above the railway bridge.)

Go up this branch, concrete at first but soon becoming rocky, and, as it enters a mature pinewood, steep! (It's for this steep bit that I mentioned sticks.) You emerge onto a gorse slope with a lacework of paths — any one of them will lead you up to the rocks below the cross. There is a variety of little paths up the rocks but the easiest turns left just before another little wood and deposits you at the foot of the cross (197 m). Relax; you've done the serious climbing. Great views; the rollers breaking on Bray beach, the curve of the bay to Killiney Hill (Walk 8) and ships out to sea. As you turn to look inland, the view is filled by the triple-topped Little (but it's higher than you are) Sugar Loaf (Walk 22) and the cone of the Great Sugar Loaf (Walk 25) with a distant backdrop of the Wicklow Mountains. Your way ahead is plain — a winding track along the broad crest of the ridge south. Two more little quartzite domes to your right — if you enjoy scrambling include them — delightful rock to climb on. All the rock round here is quartzite — very ancient, very hard.

Descend to the track, squeeze round the end of the barrier or climb easily over it (it's to stop animals, not humans) and follow it. There are short cuts — easily visible but unsuitable for those in shorts (or stockings) unless you enjoy gorse prickles. The track is incorrect on the OS map but obvious on the ground. If in doubt keep left where you've good views down to the railway and the sea (an occasional piercing railway whistle to remind you that civilisation is near). After a kilometre or so you climb a little and emerge onto a plateau. There is a fence on your left, with rocks placed handily to help you climb it. When I was last there there was a legal notice designed to protect the farmer on the landward side from being sued if you break your ankle on his property. You are more likely (but still most unlikely!) to do this on the steep little descent on the seaward side of the fence! After 50 m or so the path becomes grassy and diagonals down easily southward to the coast. When you reach a track leading from some houses down to the cliff path, turn left and follow it. (If it is still there you will be as intrigued as I was by a steel post with a standard yellow diamond road sign on it. Go and look at it — whoever put it up has a peculiar sense of humour!)

Once on the cliff path, you can't go wrong; and in spite of the notice that now confronts you, I've never heard of anyone being hit by falling rock. It is a fine walk, and you will soon see the power of the sea, even against this rocky coast. The path suddenly diverts uphill, because the original path has simply collapsed, and you can see ahead a railway tunnel, abandoned when a section of cliff complete with rail track fell into the sea, forcing the railway company to excavate a new track and tunnel out of the cliff further inshore. A fine walk — gulls and other seabirds flying, wheeling and screaming, breaking waves lashing the slabs and pinnacles of rock (slate down here), small fishing boats offshore, cormorants poised ready to dive. Evocative names along here too — Brandy Hole, Periwinkle Rocks, Crab Rock. Some forty minutes' easy walking brings you back to where you left the cliff path to climb the Head, and so back to busy Bray.

Note: The first kilometre of the Cliff Path from Bray is passable by wheelchair, enough to see some of the fine cliff scenery.

Bray Head

Carrigoona — Rocky Valley

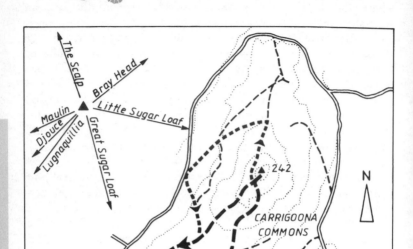

Distance: 2 km (short), 3 km (long)
Ascent: 60 m
Time: ½ hour (short), ¾ hour (long) — excluding viewing time!
Equipment: OS Discovery Sheet 56. Trainers.

As you can see, this is a very short walk, but it really is an extraordinarily pleasant one. Carrigoona Commons is a name I'd never heard of until I saw it on the new map; as far as I, or anyone else, was concerned, it was the little hill on the opposite side of the Rocky Valley to the Great Sugar Loaf, and that really describes it perfectly. It is just the walk for a sunny evening any time between April and September; time yourself to reach the top say half an hour before sunset.

Coming from Dublin take the N11, the Wexford road, to Kilmacanoge where you turn right onto the R755 signposted Glendalough. After 2 km fork right again onto the R760, signposted Enniskerry, and almost immediately take a *very* sharp turn right up a steep little hill. Park in a lay-by where the road levels out.

Now you can see your Mount Everest to the right. A good track leads away from the road (the start is hidden behind a bank) and you can follow this or (better) one of the smaller variants along the ridge overlooking the Rocky Valley. There is quartzite rock underfoot, under shallow soil, so it is good walking along dry paths with heather on either side, and no bog. Sometimes the motorcyclists practising on the steep slopes of the Rocky Valley can be heard, but fortunately they don't seem to bother about the easy slopes that we are climbing. There are fine views as the evening sun catches the grey-white rock of the Sugar Loaf while the shadows sharpen the features of the small crags that edge the valley.

As you approach the summit, the path steepens almost to a scramble, and then flattens to the cairn (242 m). Now you can admire the views! To the east the Little Sugar Loaf (Walk 22) is full in the sun; to the west the red sun is dropping down to disappear behind the big hills of the main ranges of the Wicklow Mountains — Maulin (Walk 23), Djouce and even distant Lugnaquillia. North, you can look down at the shadowed Dargle valley (Walk 18), and beyond, the great cleft of the Scalp (Walk 14).

The sun will go down, and the chill will drive you down. Either return by the way you came, or for a little extra exercise, turn right at the bottom of the steep bit and pick up a track leading north. Just before a rock outcrop, turn left onto a track heading south-west back to the road (a very quiet one), which you can follow back to your car. Or if, like me, you hate road walking, another track heading south-east brings you back onto your ascent route.

To finish off a pleasant evening, there is a friendly pub at Kilmacanoge on your homeward road.

The Little Sugar Loaf

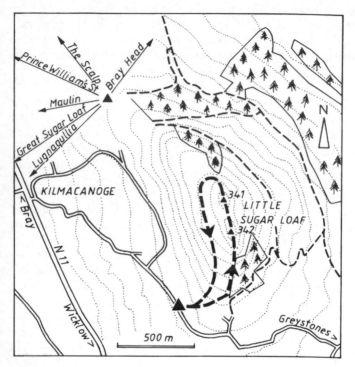

Distance: 2.3 km
Ascent: 180 m
Time: 1 hour
Equipment: OS Discovery Sheet 56. Boots, unless you like scrambling over scree in trainers, weather gear, sticks useful.

As you drive the M11 past Bray, you see three hills ahead, getting higher from Bray Head on the left through the Little Sugar Loaf to the Great Sugar Loaf on the right. Bray Head with its multiple bumps isn't great to look at (though see Walk 20), but the two Sugar Loafs, standing up steep and proud, are quite conical. They are of hard, grey quartzite and are not — as many people think — volcanic cones. As the road swings you see first one, then the other, and even though I have driven that road hundreds of times, I still muddle them up when only one is visible. Anyway, it is the Little Sugar Loaf that we are climbing today. Yes, climbing: although it is only 342 m high, it is a climb. The ridge with its three summits is rough going, with sharp, jagged rock and scree — that's why I suggest boots for what is really quite an easy walk.

Coming from Dublin take the N11 to Kilmacanoge; shortly beyond the junction for Glendalough, turn left up a narrow, winding road. After a while this comes out onto open hillside and a little later, about 1.3 km from Kilmacanoge, you will find a small grass parking area on the left, and an obvious track leading up the heather and grass hillside towards our summit. (If you have to rely on a bus, then you can walk from Kilmacanoge — allow an extra thirty to forty minutes there and back.)

Walk up the track to the tattered, scrawny remains of a wood and climb up beside it. Above the wood, vegetation almost ceases and the track becomes a rough path winding over scree and small rocks, rising over a shoulder to the first of the mountain's three summits (342 m).

Now you can pause for a rest and enjoy the view. In the distance to the west are the Wicklow Mountains, whose rounded contours are a perfect backdrop for the Great Sugar Loaf, from this direction an almost regular cone. To the east you look over Bray Head to the Irish Sea, and below you is the Earl of Meath's estate. My wife has a nice story of two English ladies staying in Greystones, wanting to climb the Little Sugar Loaf, and being told to get off the bus 'at the Earl of Meath's'. They relayed this to the conductor, who duly let them off, leaving them looking desperately around for an eponymous pub!

Continue along the ridge; there is always a path of a sort, and it is worth trying to keep to it because the ridge has little rocky steps, and its flanks are steep. It isn't at all difficult if you keep to the path, and it's a delightfully airy walk, with the view to keep you company. Last winter I was up there in a gale and had no time to do anything but keep on my feet, but that's abnormal! From the third summit (341 m) the path winds down to a grassy shoulder and a stone wall. A little to your left is a corner of the wall and beside it a narrow path heads off aiming towards the Great Sugar Loaf. It soon bends round and contours easily on heathery slopes below the ridge, leading you back to join your upward track a couple of hundred metres above the road.

There is no reason why you shouldn't reverse this route if you like to have your high point at the end of the walk; when mounting the track from the road, the turn-off onto the contouring track is just above a little cutting on the upward track.

Back to Kilmacanoge for refreshment!

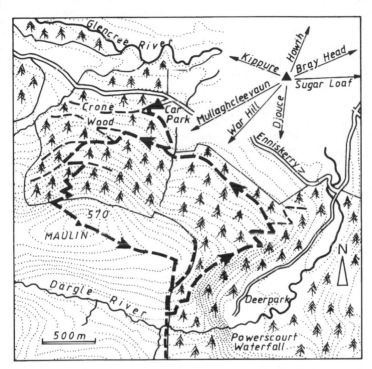

Distance: 7 km
Ascent: 500 m
Time: 2½ hours
Equipment: OS Discovery Sheet 56. Boots, weather gear, compass if the
weather is doubtful.

*This is a remarkably easy way of getting to a high viewpoint and it has
some fine valley views as well. You are on a path almost all the way, and
most of the climb and descent is easy-angled. The car park at Crone,
where you start, is generally crowded, so if you are going out on a
Sunday, I'd recommend a morning walk!*

Take the R760 south from Enniskerry. After about 3 km turn sharp right at a road signposted to Powerscourt. This road descends to the Estate entrance and then climbs to contour the south slope of Glencree. Crone car park is on the left, about 2 km beyond the Powerscourt entrance.

Go past the forest barrier and almost immediately turn left up a narrow path which soon leads you onto another forest road. This saves a walk along the road. Memorise the top end of this short cut — you'll want to use it on the way back. Turn left along the forest road which climbs steadily and then swings sharply to the right. Almost immediately after the bend there is a junction with a Wicklow Way Yellow Man marker. That is the way you'll descend, so wave at it and continue straight on. Where the mature wood on your left ends, take a narrow path which winds up to an old road. Go right to join a new road which slants uphill. If you had missed the narrow path you could have reached here by following the road, but it's a good bit longer.

Now keep following the forest road uphill. There are several junctions; go straight through the first two, turn left uphill at the third, and right uphill at the fourth. Then it is just a succession of zigzags on a deteriorating track to the top of the wood, a stile, and a post adjuring you not to light fires, ride bicycles or do other bad deeds — you are entering the Wicklow National Park. Most of the way up the hill to that point you have been in the open — there has been a lot of felling — with fine views across Glencree and back to the Great Sugar Loaf (Walk 25). I checked the route on a sunny, showery day in July, with the air so clear that every detail of the fields, farms and woods in the valley could be picked out, and the Sugar Loaf, nearly bare of heather since the heath fires of 1994, looked as if it was speckled with snow.

Cross a rough track paralleling the forest fence and pick up a stony path that winds uphill through heather. It deteriorates and grows branches; keep to the steepest — the others are really only sheep tracks. Eventually it dies out below a rock outcrop, but grass has mostly replaced the heather and it is easy to walk up the west side of the outcrop, across a shattered stone wall, to pick up a path which in a minute or so brings you to the summit of Maulin, 570 m (*Malainn*, Hill Brow).

Truly a wonderful place to be on a fine day. The view swings all the way round from Howth (Walk 4), past Dalkey (Walk 8), Bray Head (Walk 20) and the Sugar Loafs (Walks 22 and 25) to the mass of Djouce and War Hill. The last day I was there the sea was ultramarine blue, the sky a lighter blue near the horizon, deepening towards the apogee, flecked with brilliant clouds, with the near-perfect cone of the Sugar Loaf standing up proudly in the foreground.

The way down is obvious — a clear path winding down a little south of east. It starts almost at the cairn, so would be hard to miss even in mist; if you are in doubt, a rough compass bearing will put you right. Follow the wide path, rather stony (please keep to it and don't widen it more!), to a rough track and turn right downhill beside the forest. Soon the River Dargle comes in sight, but just before the slope eases you will see another park sign, and then a Wicklow Way marker. Turn left into the wood; now you are on the Way with no more navigation problems.

A few minutes through the wood and the Way takes you along the side of the Powerscourt Deerpark. It is a gently sloping path, soft underfoot, with fine views of the waterfall beside and below you. The path turns into the forest and becomes a forest road, zigzags, and then takes you on a long, level walk back to that junction we noted on the outward journey and, reversing our outward steps, we return to the car park.

The nearest refreshments are in Enniskerry.

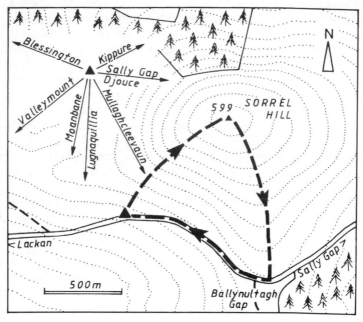

Distance: 3 km (2 km returning same way)
Ascent: 200 m
Time: 1¼ to 1½ hours
Equipment: OS Discovery Sheet 56. Boots (trainers in summer if dry), compass, if the weather is doubtful.

Sorrel Hill (599 m) is a typical round-topped Wicklow granite hill, isolated from the main range of the Wicklow Mountains by the Ballydonnell and upper Liffey valleys. Though only a short climb from the road running to Ballynultagh Gap to the south, its isolation makes it a good, relatively accessible viewing point.

Take the N81 to Blessington. In the town at the pedestrian lights turn left (signposted Kilbride). A kilometre down this road take a righthand turn to cross a bridge over Pollaphuca Reservoir, then turn right again. About 5 km from Blessington along this road is the tiny village of Lackan — fork left at the shop and follow the road up between high banks past scattered houses until it suddenly emerges onto the open hillside. Eight hundred metres further on the road bends gently right and there is room for several cars to park at a cutting on the left, which marks the start of the walk.

This part of the hillside is extensively grazed by sheep and sometimes cattle. It is a popular walking area, and is also used on occasion by mountain bikers and horse trekkers. Motorbike trials are sometimes held here, and when the wind is from the north-west the slopes below the road may be busy with hang-gliders. It can be a very busy place but most of the time it is unusual to meet more than one or two other walkers. All this activity, however, means there is a multitude of small paths, so the walking is quite easy. Pick any path that is heading uphill and you will eventually arrive at the summit. The grassy lower slopes give way to heather growing on peat, but at the top much of the peat has been washed away, exposing the underlying granite sand and stones bleached white by the acidic, peaty groundwater. The actual high point is unmarked but a few metres to the north-west is an imposing cairn — a pile of loose stones heaped up on top of an older, much more substantial structure.

Many of the hills along the western edge of the Wicklow Mountains, particularly those that jut out westward, have substantial stone structures which in many cases are sited just off the true summit, seemingly the better to overlook the land below. On Seefin and Seefingan, rising just across the Liffey valley to the north, and on Seahan (Walk 15) further north, there are megalithic tombs. To the south, Black Hill, Moanbane and Silsean are set back overlooking Pollaphuca Reservoir and have bare summits. Further south, Slieve Corragh and Church Mountain are also topped by large, ruined, stone mounds.

Beyond the Reservoir, formed in 1942 by damming the River Liffey to provide hydroelectric power, the Central Plain stretches away into the haze. To the east is Kippure with its television masts, Sally Gap, and the main spine of the Wicklow Mountains, culminating in Mullaghcleevaun, the second highest mountain of the range (Walk 30).

You can descend the same way — simple enough unless in mist, when a direction between south and south-west will bring you back to the road (235° direct to the car). To take the longer way round, head south-eastward to find a path leading through the peat banks and onto rather wet, heathery ground sloping down towards Ballynultagh Gap. I have never been able to follow this path the whole way to the Gap: it disappears and reappears among the heather and should not be relied on as a navigation aid. In good visibility, the white scar of the track heading up Black Hill opposite makes a good mark — aim a little to the left of its lower end. In mist, a bearing of 180° leads direct to the Gap. It can be rough going here, and there are very few paths. On the way you may pass some old, abandoned heaps of turf cut from the nearby banks and left to dry. The traces of a path between two half-buried lines of stones running some way up the hill towards the turf-cuttings may be vestiges of an old turf-cutters' track.

When you come to the road turn right and it is about 1 km back to the car. A road is not normally the best finish to a hill walk but this is pleasant — wide, grassy verges, fine views over the reservoir, and hardly any traffic unless you have picked a day when all the other users of the hillside are about. Lackan, with a pleasant pub, is less than 3 km before you.

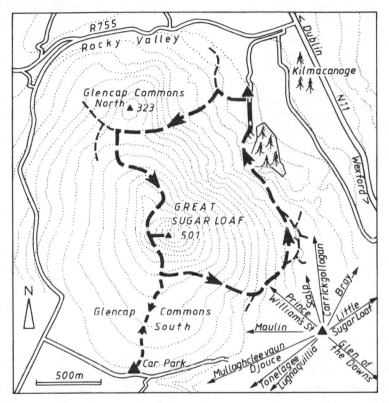

Distance: 2.4 km (short), 5.3 km (long)
Ascent: 200 m (short), 380 m (long)
Time: ¾ to 1 hour (short), 2¼ hours (long)
Equipment: OS Discovery Sheet 56. Boots, weather gear, sticks useful.

The Great Sugar Loaf is a must. If you head south from Dublin by either the Bray or Enniskerry roads, its symmetrical cone dominates the view. Little and Great have quite similar profiles, and when the Little alone is in view it is possible to confuse them, but once the Great comes in sight its profile is unmistakable. A big heather fire a few years ago exposed the bare, white, quartzite rocks and scree so that from a distance it appeared the mountain was snow-covered. Now the vegetation is gradually recovering. It is climbed probably more frequently than any other mountain in Ireland except Croagh Patrick (which has the unfair advantage of being a holy mountain). I have to say that although I've seen three-year-olds and eighty-year-olds on it, it is not that easy. Like its Little brother it is formed of hard, quartzite rock and, even on the easiest route, the climb to the summit is over scree and broken rock; hands will be needed as well as feet, especially when descending.

I describe two routes: the short, popular one, suitable for peak-baggers, or a quick snap of exercise; and the longer one, a fine, quite challenging walk, which makes a complete ring round the mountain, with a dash up to the summit.

The approach for both is the same; take the Wexford road (N11) as far as Kilmacanoge. Turn right up the R755 and (for the short route) follow it as it climbs through the Rocky Valley and round the side of the Sugar Loaf until the road levels out. Take the first turn left and in less than a kilometre, stop in the car park on the left.

There is no difficulty in finding the way — a broad, braided track heads straight for the summit from the car park. If you are lucky you may see a hare or two, and if you are clearing the head after Christmas they'll be in winter trim. Rising gently at first, the track steepens and then levels out on the western slope of the summit cone. Now turn right and climb the obvious much-travelled route up steep scree and broken rock to the summit (501 m).

There's a fine view all round. Working clockwise from the north-east, we have the town of Bray, Bray Head (Walk 20) peeping over the Little Sugar Loaf (Walk 22), backed by the Irish Sea; then the gash of the Glen of the Downs, a glacial overflow channel. Far in the south-west, Lugnaquillia should be visible. Running northwards, the big peaks of the backbone of Wicklow: Camaderry, Tonelagee (Walk 32), Mullaghcleevaun (Walk 30), with Djouce, Maulin (Walk 23) and Prince William's Seat (Walk 16) in front. Then, nearly north, is another glacier-cut gash, the Scalp (Walk 14) and finally the Lead Mines chimney and Carrickgollogan (Walk 13).

After all that it is something of a disappointment to descend the same way, though on many days, even in summer, you may be glad to escape from the windy summit.

Now for the longer route which is almost all on tracks or paths; the only problem is that there are many paths — care is needed to be on the right one! At Kilmacanoge turn as before onto the R755 but almost immediately, just before a shop, turn left up a narrow road signposted to the John Fitzsimons GAA Club. The road is twisty so take it slowly, and there is quite a lot of residential traffic. Just before the GAA clubhouse park on the verge — plenty of room.

The OS map is choosy in the paths it marks so I am giving you a careful description. Go along a path between the fences of the GAA and a private house. This brings you in a minute or two to open hillside. The path bears right and, climbing gently, crosses a small stream; beyond the stream turn sharply left and follow a path which winds up beside the stream. After a bit it swings away north but then settles down to climb quite steeply up a grass and heather slope towards the long, level saddle between the Sugar Loaf and point 323 to the north (this section of the path is easily visible from below). Approaching the flat surface of the saddle the path almost disappears but keep going and when you meet a broad track (shown on the map) turn left and follow the track as it climbs steadily and swings left around a hump on the ridge, then swings back a little to pass onto the western slope of the summit cone. Here you join the short route to clamber up the steep slope to the summit.

On descent take the short route, first down the scree and then left along the broad track towards the south. Where the slope eases the track crosses an earth bank. Turn left along this until it peters out. There is a path leading downhill; it is initially not very clear (it's on the OS map all the same!) but if you aim towards the Glen of the Downs you'll soon find it, very obvious through bracken. If in doubt, keep aiming towards the Glen and in five or six minutes you'll meet a clear path diagonalling across the slope. Turn left along it and your navigational problems, if we can dignify them as such, are over. The path turns and descends steeply until it reaches flatter ground; it improves and keeps along the foot of the slope. Keep right at a fork as you approach a small wood, and soon after passing the wood you join a paved road; your car will be in sight in a very few minutes.

I find this a very satisfying walk, and you can quench your well-earned thirst in Kilmacanoge!

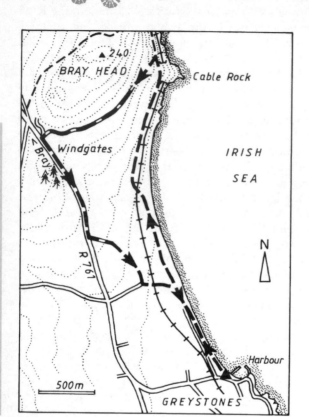

Distance: 7.5 km

Ascent: 120 m

Time: 2¼ hours (at least ¼ hour extra if you start from the railway station)

Equipment: OS Discovery Sheet 56. Trainers.

Greystones is a busy small town, many of whose inhabitants commute daily to Dublin. It has fine, if rather stony, beaches, so there are plenty of cafés, pubs, take-aways and the like for visitors (and for you on your return!). You can take advantage of the good rail and bus services provided for commuters and beach visitors. The cliff path is an easy walk, on a level or well-graded surface, with fine views of the Irish Sea across the beach, and later of the rocky sea cliffs of Bray Head. If you prefer you can walk the first part on the beach among bathers and anglers, but it is rather soft going except below the high tide mark. The walk is capable of several variations, and you can actually continue to Bray. The time given above is for the standard route.

From Dublin, bus or rail will bring you to Greystones. If you are travelling by car take the N11 and then the M11 past Bray and as you climb the hill towards Kilmacanoge, fork left and go right almost immediately at a roundabout along a bypass through the southern suburbs of Bray. At the next roundabout turn right again onto the R761 which will take you into Greystones. You can park at the harbour.

The path starts as rather rough-surfaced road just above the beach and keeps along the top of the mud cliff, which, low at first, gradually increases in height and steepness. At a football field (if there's a match on there may be parked cars) you turn sharp right then left to get really close to the cliff edge. There has been some erosion here and the path is being moved shoreward. Soon you come to an imposing high bridge over a very small stream. In the nesting season (April–June) it is worth taking a track in the direction of Greystones which takes you down to the beach and a section of cliff where many sand-martins nest. If you have preferred the beach so far, here is the place to join the cliff path — access from the beach is difficult further on.

Steadily rising, the path continues along the top of the cliff; the railway, thus far on the landward side, passes under it. The near-vertical mud cliff ends and is replaced by steep slopes covered in trees and bushes. The path narrows with high undergrowth on either side — hardly room for two people to pass. The railway below is on a ledge carved out of the slope, in and out of tunnels. When a train passes, hooter blaring as it enters a tunnel, it is hardly visible through the vegetation.

Then the path emerges onto open ground, with a wall on the left. It rises over the swelling ground of the Cable Rock headland, and the sweep of cliffs and coves running away towards Bray comes into view. In stormy weather the waves beating against the slate cliffs

77

are a wonderful sight. Over the years they have beaten to some effect. One section of the railway line was washed away and a new alignment had to be constructed further inshore, with deeper cuttings and more tunnel. Very shortly a path goes up to the right, with a choice of gate or stile in the wall.

Now you have to make a decision. Continue along the cliff path to Bray (Walk 20) where the user of public transport can pick up either a bus or the DART; return the way you have come; or take another route back to Greystones. For this last, climb the stile or pass through the gate and follow the track which leads to a surfaced road. (Note in passing the road sign, fruit of someone's peculiar sense of humour.) The road, a quiet one which serves a few houses and a new block of apartments, leads you to the main Bray to Greystones road, which unfortunately has to be followed for a little more than a kilometre towards Greystones before a turning on the left can be taken. Starting as a road and then becoming a track, this leads you back down to the 'imposing bridge' that you crossed on your outward way. Return to Greystones by beach or path.

Note: The section as far as the 'imposing bridge' is passable by wheelchair.

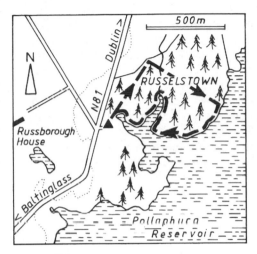

Distance: 2.5 km
Ascent: None
Time: ½ to ¾ hour
Equipment: OS Discovery Sheet 56. Trainers, or better, boots because bits are muddy.

This is a short, woodland walk beside the Pollaphuca Reservoir, formed when the River Liffey was dammed at Pollaphuca in 1942, to generate electricity and to provide a greater water supply for Dublin than the Vartry Reservoirs (Walk 31) near Roundwood could supply. The reservoir seems more like a natural lake, and there are fine views across the water to meadows and rolling hills. The wood holds a variety of wildlife, while the reservoir is host in winter to grey-lag geese and many species of duck. A curiosity on the OS map is the Wicklow–Kildare county boundary zigzagging down the middle of the reservoir, following the bed of the river in pre-reservoir days! This is a short walk but could well be a leg-stretcher during a circuit of the reservoir by car.

Take the N81 out of Dublin and 3.5 km beyond Blessington is a righthand junction leading to Russborough House. (You could also reach here by the number 65 bus.) Opposite is an entrance leading into Russelstown forest. Take the road through this entrance and park at the broad space almost immediately inside the gate, at the head of an inlet of the reservoir. The road continues along the southern shore of the inlet to a slipway and moorings, much used by anglers and other boaters (but note that a permit is needed for either activity). Beyond the slipway, when the level of the lake is low, fragments of old walls and a chimney pot mark the site of Russelstown House, from which the wood gets its name.

However, this walk follows another forest road (closed to wheeled traffic by a bar) which heads northward from the parking area, crossing the small stream which flows into the inlet before entering the forest. This is the remains of an old road which ran down to a busy junction at Burgage, now under water. Step over the barrier and follow the road into the forest. The trees are a mixture of spruce, pine and larch, part of the strip of forest planted all around the lake by the Electricity Supply Board in the late fifties. If you go quietly you are likely to see a squirrel or two or a few deer — other animals frequenting the wood are harder to spot — and many birds may be heard among the treetops. Soon you come to a row of magnificent old beech, oak and ash trees alongside the road. At the last of these, an ash tree (it is not necessary to know anything about trees as this tree is identified by a small label, 'Ash *Fraxinus excelsior*'), a rough logging track heads off to the right into the larch forest. Leave the road here and follow the track down to a bridge over another small stream.

Cross the bridge and follow the track in the same easterly direction. Ignore the deep ruts of other logging tracks heading off to either side and stay with the track until it passes out of the larches into spruce forest and comes to an end under a long-dead elm tree. Straight ahead you will already be able to glimpse the lake beyond the trees; continuing in the same direction, pick your way through the forest to emerge onto the lake shore.

Across the lake the high mountains are hidden behind Baltyboys Hill and the views are all of water and low, rounded hills and farmland. When you reach the lake shore turn to the right to follow it back around towards the starting point. As this is a reservoir the water level is very variable. When it is low, a broad shingle beach makes easy walking; at high water, you must thread your way along small paths between the lake and the forest, among the alders and willows which grow by the water's edge. Soon the slipway and inlet come into view, but the way is barred by another small inlet, often occupied by a heron or a pair of swans which will flap away as you appear round the corner. Follow a steadily improving small path along the shore of this little bay until it is possible to cross the small stream which feeds it. When the level of the lake is high it may be necessary to go right up to the bridge crossed on the outward trip, but at lower water levels the stream is an easy jump, though be wary of bog. Wherever you cross the stream, turn to the left and follow a small path by the edge of the lake back around to the track just 100 m from the starting point.

If you need refreshment, about 3 km further south on the main road is Poulaphouca House, on the right just after the dam. (Or there are many establishments in Blessington.) The building on the other side of the road at Pollaphuca was the terminal of the tramway which once ran here from Dublin.

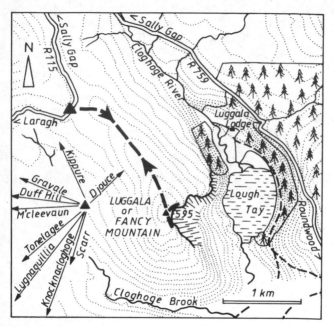

Distance: 4 km
Ascent: 110 m
Time: 1½ hours (excluding viewing time!)
Equipment: OS Discovery Sheet 56. Boots, weather gear, compass if the weather is uncertain.

This is a short, straight-out-and-back route, and the actual walking is rather dull and a bit boggy underfoot, but I've included it for the magnificent, plunging view which greets you as you reach the top of Fancy Mountain, for the feeling of wilderness in the middle of the Wicklow Hills, and for the wide views of those same hills.

Take the R115 out of Dublin, along the Military Road over the Featherbed and past the head of Glencree and the two Lough Brays (see Walk 19 for more information about the Military Road). The road climbs steeply up, passes the entrance to the road to the television masts on Kippure, then winds round open bogland, the source of the River Liffey which flows out far to the west onto the Central Plain before turning round to flow through Dublin. At the Sally Gap crossroads you meet one of the few roads which cross the Wicklow Mountains — take note for your return journey. Now you continue along the Military Road (signposted here for Laragh) which curls round spurs and re-entrants to stop at a car park about 2.5 km from the Sally Gap. It is really bare and wild up here (though the road is busy enough on a Sunday!) and it is easy to see why this was one of the last haunts of the 1798 'rebels', and why the Military Road was built to flush them out. Actually it was hardly finished before Michael Dwyer, the last of them, was transported to Australia.

Leaving the car park, cross the road, and a few metres back towards the Sally Gap, find a rough path across the bog, heading east along the crest — if you can call the top of such a broad, swelling ridge a 'crest'. The path may be wet, but not enough to worry any reasonable type of walking boot. Wet or dry, follow the path as it meanders across the bog, through masses of purple heather, and climbs to the summit of Fancy Mountain (595 m) — an attractive name for which I can't find an origin.

Just beyond the summit the ground drops away in a tremendous cliff, nearly 350 m high, which stretches away on both sides in a curve embracing Lough Tay. At the head of the lake is a grassy alluvial plain graced by a small, domed, white temple, and behind, hidden in the trees, a house — Luggala Lodge — belonging to Garech Browne of the Guinness family. Turn right and you look down the valley of the Cloghoge River to boomerang-shaped Lough Dan, with steep, wooded slopes above its east shore. Raise your eyes and everywhere around are hills: as you swing round from Djouce in the north-east past Scarr, Knocknacloghoge, Lugnaquillia distant to the south, Tonelagee (Walk 32), Mullaghcleevaun (Walk 30) and the row of tops beside the Military Road to Kippure to the north-west.

There is a path along the top of the cliff and it is worth walking along a bit in either direction, especially to the north above the Luggala Crag, one of the two finest rock-climbing crags in Wicklow.

It would be nice to find a way down to the lake and up to the road on the far side, but firstly the only path is exceedingly steep and dangerous and secondly the owner is besieged with Sunday strollers from that road and I'm not going to add to his troubles. So I hope 'the game has been worth the candle' because I am going to tell you to walk back the way you came. You *could* turn south, descend to the Cloghoge *Brook* and climb Knocknacloghoge beyond it. Be careful if you do! Crossing the valley one winter day when the snow lay deep, I heard a shout and looked back — no sign of my wife! Eventually she climbed out of a hole between rocks deep enough to engulf her whole height. Fortunately she was unhurt. Beyond Knocknacloghoge a forest road will lead out to the Military Road and eventually to your car, but timewise that is well beyond the scope of this guide!

When you reach your car it is worth turning right at Sally Gap and following the road which takes you high above the eastern shore of Lough Tay, with an equally stunning view of the lake and the cliffs on which you stood an hour or so before. If your previous exertions have not exhausted you, it is worth walking 100 m or so from the road to get the best view of the lake and the climbers' crag.

To get back to Dublin, continue along the road which turns east, passes one junction and a crossroads, and debouches onto the R755 which will bring you to Kilmacanoge, the N11 and Dublin.

The J.B. Malone Memorial from Ballinastoe

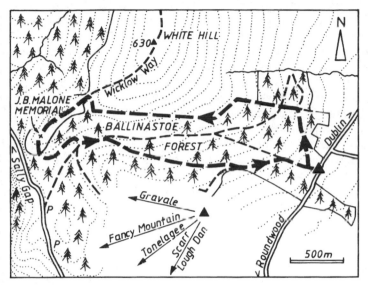

Distance: 6 km
Ascent: 270 m
Time: 2¼ hours
Equipment: OS Discovery Sheet 56. Boots, weather gear.

J.B. Malone was one of the great pioneers of Irish hill walking. His weekly articles for many years in the Evening Herald *probably brought more Dubliners into walking than any other factor. In his later years as Field Officer of the Long Distance Walking Routes Committee he was able to fulfil a long-held dream of a waymarked way through the Wicklow Mountains — the Wicklow Way. He is remembered by a carved stone beside a boulder on the Way, overlooking one of the best views in Wicklow — down on Lough Tay and Lough Dan and the beautiful valley that joins them. The climax of this walk is the view from his memorial stone.*

Take the Enniskerry road (R117) to Enniskerry, and then the R760, which descends steeply to Tinnehinch Bridge across the River

Dargle and then climbs up to the south. Take the second right fork onto an unclassified road (signposted Roundwood) soon after a sharp turn left. This road climbs onto a rounded ridge overlooking the Powerscourt Deerpark and Waterfall, with Maulin (Walk 23), War Hill and Djouce behind. Unfortunately trees have been planted right up to the road so it is impossible to see the waterfall unless you stop at the car park halfway along the straight and walk down the path through the wood for a few minutes until you meet a level path where trees part to reveal the waterfall in full flow — worth the diversion if you have time to spare. Stop at Ballinastoe car park 7.4 km after leaving the R760.

Go up the forest road from the entrance, past the barrier and almost immediately turn right up a good forest road with a gatepost on either side. There has been much felling, and most of the ground on your left looks like a battlefield. After about 500 m you come to an overhead electric wire on wooden posts. Turn left and follow the posts up a rough track. The road swings away to your right and comes back to meet you higher up — the short cut saves you a good half-kilometre. Leave the poles which follow the road to the left and continue straight up the track, now with trees on either side. Soon the track crosses the forest fence; there are handy stones on either side and the barbed wire has been covered with a timber so the crossing is harmless. The track continues up easily between the forest on one side and the heather slopes of White Hill and Djouce Mountain on the other. Be grateful for it, even if it is rather stony (it is a firebreak); wading through deep heather is no fun! More or less following the edge of the trees, the track climbs over the shoulder of White Hill (this is your highest point — 570 m) and curves round gently — and less stonily — to meet the Wicklow Way as it descends from White Hill. A fine view here across the trees to the main Wicklow range; like so many views, it is best morning or evening. While it can be idyllic up here, it's quite high and is pretty miserable if it's cold and wet — that's why I suggested good rain gear!

Now you join the walkers' equivalent of a motorway — well not quite, it isn't two-lane! The Wicklow Way, close to Dublin, is the most popular of the thirty or so waymarked ways in Ireland. In the sixteen years of its existence, walkers' feet have stripped the vegetation of the bogland over a width of 5–10 m. The National

Park has laid a trackway of wooden sleepers for walkers to follow while the vegetation regenerates. It isn't beautiful, but it is the only practical solution and (hush!) it is a lot pleasanter to walk on than sticky wet bog! A few minutes' striding along the sleepers bring you to J.B.'s memorial under a big boulder.

Here definitely is one of Wicklow's best views. Below you is the oval Lough Tay — the house of a branch of the Guinness family (of Guinness stout fame) is hidden in the trees — while beyond it is one of Wicklow's best rock-climbing crags, Luggala. Look further right and a valley floor of meadows with steep sides leads your eye to the boomerang-shaped sweep of Lough Dan and ridge after ridge behind, culminating in Lugnaquillia, at 925 m the highest of the Wicklow Mountains. When I checked out the walk for this guide, the winter sun was shining over Scarr, pale, but strong enough to turn the brown winter heather copper red, while below windless Lough Tay mirrored the great crag behind it.

But we must move on. We follow the Way as it descends to the corner of the forest, turns left, plunges into dark woodland and emerges onto a rough track. The Yellow Man directs you right along the track, and over a stile to a real forest road. Here we turn *left* and leave the Way. I had better confess that if you turn *right,* about two minutes' walk will bring you to a car park on the Luggala road; if you really want to get to J.B.'s memorial and you haven't the time for the walk I'm describing, you can nip up from the car park and back in half an hour or so — plus viewing time.

We, however, are walking back virtuously along the forest road to Ballinastoe. It is a pleasant, easy walk. There has been much felling, but there are still stands of trees as we look down into the valley below us and beyond to the Vartry Reservoirs (Walk 31), source of much of Dublin's water. After about 600 m fork right and continue easily and gently downhill. As you near the starting point the road passes among mature trees, well spaced, rising from a grassy sward. A good place to picnic; you are near the edge of the forest so there's a view through the trees to the reservoirs. Then you pass the battlefield on your left, meet your outward road, and are back at the car park.

The J.B. Malone Memorial from Ballinastoe

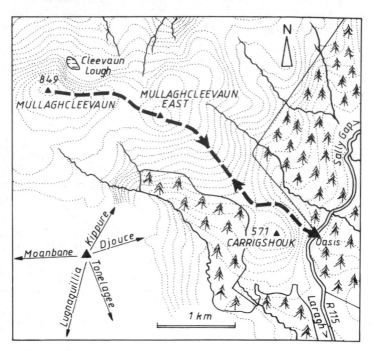

Distance: 8.5 km

Ascent: 480 m

Time: 3½ hours

Equipment: OS Discovery Sheet 56. Boots, weather gear, compass if weather is uncertain.

What, you may ask, is the Oasis? It is a small dell of mature trees, once the only wood for miles and well known to every Wicklow walker, but now nearly lost in the modern plantations.

This is an up-and-down route and longer than any other in this book. So why include it? Well, it is the easiest way to the second highest of the Wicklow Mountains, and is right in the middle of really wild country with fine views all round. There are some vague paths, navigation isn't difficult, and with a little care, it is not unpleasant underfoot. Unless

*the weather is really good, be sure to have your map and compass: the
summit area can cloud up easily.*

Coming from Dublin follow the Military Road R115 from
Rathfarnham over the Featherbed. After the 1798 Rebellion, this
road was driven right through the middle of the mountains in order
to flush out the fighters who had taken refuge in this wild area. As
the road winds down into the head of Glencree, you can glimpse
through the trees the first of the series of military barracks along the
Road. It is now a Reconciliation Centre. Continue past the two
Lough Brays (Walk 19) and the Sally Gap crossroads and park in
one of the lay-bys near the end of the forestry on the right of the
road, some 8 km from the Sally Gap crossroads; the steep, rocky
point 571 (Carrigshouk) looms above you.

Leave the road at the end of the forest, and strike diagonally
uphill to the left. With any kind of luck you'll find a path while
contouring under Carrigshouk. Follow this path, or if you don't find
it, one of the numerous sheep tracks, until you can diagonal up to
the saddle between Carrigshouk and Mullaghcleevaun East. Keep
along the middle of the saddle (there is a bit of a path) to avoid
crossing the boggy gullies which run off either side, and then climb
steadily up to Cleevaun East — the fence is easy to cross — no
barbed wire! When the summit comes in view, bear a little right for
the best going underfoot. A small cairn (795 m) among big rocks
confirms your arrival. Pause and study the way ahead to
Mullaghcleevaun (*Mullach Cliabháin*, Summit of the Basket). A
little foresight will find you a route that is over short grass, dry bog
or granite gravel. There is a vague path much of the way, but this is
not visible at a distance. Once you are up the steep — well, relatively
steep — bit, you have another 300–400 m walking on short grass to
the summit triangulation pillar (849 m). You can shelter behind a
rock — there is one for every wind direction! — while you eat your
well-earned lunch.

From the summit you can appreciate the wilderness of the
Wicklow Mountains. Hills of heather, grass and bog surround you
wherever you look. To the north they stretch to the masts on
Kippure; to the east the sea can be seen very distantly beyond
Djouce; to the south there are hills upon hills to Lugnaquillia, the

only spot higher than where you stand. Only to the west, over Moanbane, can you see the plains of West Wicklow and Kildare. Make sure to go to the north edge of the plateau and look down on small Cleevaun Lough, tucked into a rocky coum (the 'basket' of the name?). On a big rock there is a plaque commemorating three An Óige members who drowned off Port Oriel — their friends must have known they'd appreciate this view.

Return by the same route. If you've been wandering round on the plateau, take care to leave it in the same direction as you came from! (This is where a compass may be useful!) Once you establish the direction of Cleevaun East (about 115°, a little south of east), you should have no difficulty finding an easy way back — if you were careful to note landmarks on your way up. As you descend from Cleevaun East towards the saddle, a long, white boulder at the foot of the slope to Carrigshouk is a good point to aim for. Just before reaching it, swerve off down towards the forest on your left and pick up the path or a sheep track to bring you past Carrigshouk and back to the road.

You can either return by your outward route or continue along the Military Road past the impressive Glenmacnass Waterfall to Laragh (food and drink available) and return to Dublin by the R755 and N11.

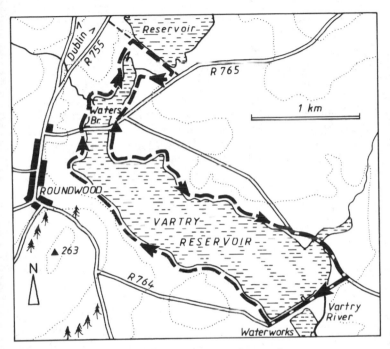

Distance: 6 5 km south of the Causeway, 2.5 km north
Ascent: Minimal!
Time: South 1¾ hours, north ¾ hour
Equipment: OS Discovery Sheet 56. Trainers (boots, even gumboots for the north in winter).

The Lower Vartry Reservoir was built in the latter part of the nineteenth century and, with the more recent Upper Reservoir, is a major source of water for Dublin, Dun Laoghaire, Bray and Wicklow. The Vartry River (Abhainn Fheartraí) rises in the Calary bog south of the Great Sugar Loaf (Walk 25) and after passing through the reservoirs continues through the Devil's Glen (Walk 34) and empties into the Broad Lough north of Wicklow town. The Lower Reservoir is divided in two by a road bridge (the Causeway) which serves as a good starting point. The southern, longer, section has a good footpath running right round it. The path round the northern section (which also includes the dam for the Upper Reservoir) is muddier and includes a stream crossing which is sometimes impracticable — more of that later on. This is an easy walk (no hills), popular on Sundays, and there is plenty here for the bird-watcher.

Take the N11 out of Dublin, turn onto the R755 and just as you enter Roundwood turn left on the R765 which brings you very quickly to the Causeway (Waters Bridge on the OS map), which you cross to the far side where a gate and stone stile can be seen on the south (right) side. It is possible to park on the verge, but you may prefer to park in Roundwood (add ten minutes each way to your time). This walk can also be done using the St Kevin's bus to Glendalough.

Cross the wall and walk the path which follows the shore. The actual water line will depend on the season — the reservoir will shrink considerably most summers — in fact one year I saw sheep grazing on grass which had sprung up well below the winter water level! The path meanders along through a narrow belt of pine between the shore and the boundary wall; it's a bit muddy in places but pleasant walking. The shore is ill-defined with rocks and reed beds. This is a good place for bird-watching — mallard, water-hens, and a colleague reports seeing a pair of great crested grebes. After about half an hour the path joins a minor road which momentarily leaves the reservoir shore and then meets a bigger road. Turn right and in a couple of minutes you are on the top of the reservoir dam. There are several items of interest — the tower of the water take-off, the ponds of the waterworks below and (unique in Ireland?) a 'Public Convenience' in the middle of the country. At the other end of the dam another stone stile takes you onto the drier and more open path along the southern shore and back to the Causeway you started from — but at the Roundwood end.

Now for the chancy bit. Climb the gate opposite to gain the path which meanders along, rather muddily, through a narrow belt of mixed woodland. When I did a final check on this walk the reservoir was very high; the trees were up to their knees in water, the water was absolutely still and you couldn't tell tree trunk from reflection! After a few minutes you reach a stream coming in from your left, small except after heavy rain when it may be a torrent. It will probably be crossable, almost certainly if you are wearing rubber boots. If you don't like it, turn back (I did) — it's only a few minutes.

If you can cross, you soon come to the head of the reservoir — a swamp of reeds among birch trees — where you may find reed warblers. The path continues on to the foot of a grassy bank, actually the upper reservoir dam, which you should climb to its broad crest. The sudden view is stunning; you've been among trees, now you are on a high ridge with a vista across the water edged by trees narrowing in the distance, culminating in the Great Sugar Loaf. Turn right and walk to the end of the dam passing the water take-off with its lattice bridge. You may have company here — an evening stroll along the dam (there's a road at either end) seems popular locally. Continue beyond the end of the dam until you meet the track from the entrance gate. Turn right onto the muddy road and almost immediately leave it for a path on the left leading to stone steps which bring you down beside the impressive masonry outlet structure. Below you is the vertical-sided outlet channel, cut deep out of solid rock, the water running fast, turbulent and noisy.

Follow the path beside the channel; the notices warning of 'steep slopes' are rather overstated, but when the autumn leaves are lying damp and slippery on the path a little care is advisable. At the same time of year, pause and look carefully into the channel; this is when the trout from the lake come up into the channel to spawn. They are hard to see but if you notice some stones on the bed whiter than others, you may well see a trout, whose swishing tail fins have cleaned the stone while she dug in the bed to lay her eggs. You may see heron also — they are better at seeing trout than you are! Soon you come to the open water and the path climbs a little and twists along, on a high bank above the shore, close to the boundary wall, quite different to the other flat shore, whose fringe of reeds and trees is easily visible. Ten minutes or so from the dam brings you back through a green gate to your starting point.

If you had to turn back from the stream, it is worth crossing the Causeway to go through the green gate nearly opposite your start. Then reverse the description just above and go up to the upper dam — worth it for the outlet channel and the vista from the dam.

Now back to Roundwood for bus, car — or refreshment!

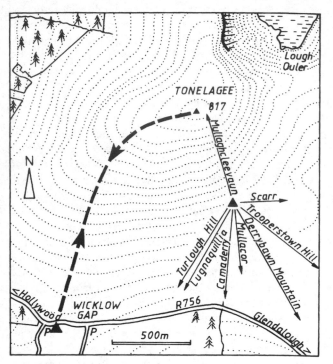

Tonelagee from Wicklow Gap

Distance: 4 km
Ascent: 350 m
Time: 2–2¼ hours
Equipment: OS Map 56. Boots, weather gear, compass if weather is uncertain.

The road between Glendalough and Hollywood crosses the mountains at Wicklow Gap, where it rises to 470 m on the southern slopes of Tonelagee (817 m) and makes a good starting point for a relatively short walk to the top of the third highest mountain in the range. This can be a very pleasant trip on a clear summer's evening. The views from the summit are vast, but I have been there when snow lay deeper than the heather, and bitter wind and driving snow made the conditions almost

Arctic. It's wise to check the weather forecast before starting out, and go equipped accordingly. Its Irish name, Tóin le Gaoth, *'Backside to the Wind', can be very apposite!*

From the eastern side of the mountains take the road towards Glendalough (R756) out of Laragh for 1.5 km, then fork to the right up the Glendasan valley (for more detail see Walk 33, Turlough Hill). This is the route taken by an ancient way known as St Kevin's Road which ran from the village of Hollywood across Wicklow Gap to the shrine of St Kevin in Glendalough. About 6.5 km up the valley, just below the summit of the Gap, pass a road running down to the left towards the lower part of Turlough Hill power station, and park in the car park on the left. Approaching from the west, turn off the N81 about 10 km beyond Blessington onto the R756, go through Hollywood and up the Kings River valley for about 18 km to the Gap. Just over the top, and beyond a turn-off to the right which climbs up to the reservoir on top of Turlough Hill, is the car park.

Cross the road and go straight up the hill — it is wet, heather-covered bog at first, making it hard to get started without wet feet. A path goes through this stretch but it is not much of an improvement. Soon the slope steepens and heather gives way to grass. It is better to go straight upward rather than veering off to the right on the direct line to the summit, where rocky slopes grown over with heather make the going difficult. The grass slopes may seem long, but eventually you reach the first peat hags which show you are coming near to the easier angle of the ridge that runs south-westward from the top of Tonelagee. Continue uphill and gradually bear right until you are on the ridge. Now you can stride out over the dry peat covered with stunted heather and many small rocks, the broad ridge seeming like the roof of Wicklow. Soon you come to a group of very large boulders which provide excellent shelter from wind and rain. Until recently there was a heather bed here left by a bivouacker. A few metres further on, the summit (817 m) is marked by a ruinous cairn topped by a triangulation pillar.

Broad and rounded, the summit provides expansive rather than dramatic views. To the north the main spine of the range stretches out to Mullaghcleevaun (Walk 30) and beyond towards Kippure with its television mast. Round to the east are Djouce and

Scarr with the sea beyond. Glendasan can be seen dropping towards the Avonmore valley, and just to the right of this behind Camaderry are the mountains above Glendalough — Mullacor and Lugduff. The bulk of Lugnaquillia and its offshoots dominates the view to the south, behind the artificial lake on top of Turlough Hill. Westward the view reaches over towards the lowlands.

Some 300 m north-east of the summit, hidden by the convex slope, are high crags overlooking the corrie lake of Lough Ouler. On a fine day it worth walking north along the ridge towards Stoney Top for a few minutes to get a glimpse of the lake. The further you descend, the better the view of this typical coum, carved out by an Ice Age hanging glacier — but of course the more you have to climb back. In mist the crags are a potential danger, but the descent route is in the opposite direction, returning down the ridge to the west. When the clouds are down it is not easy to find the best place to veer left off the ridge towards the Gap. Accurate map and compass work is useful here, but if you head between south and south-west from the summit or high on the ridge you will come to the Wicklow Gap road, and the worst you will meet is some rough, ankle-threatening terrain and an unnecessary road walk.

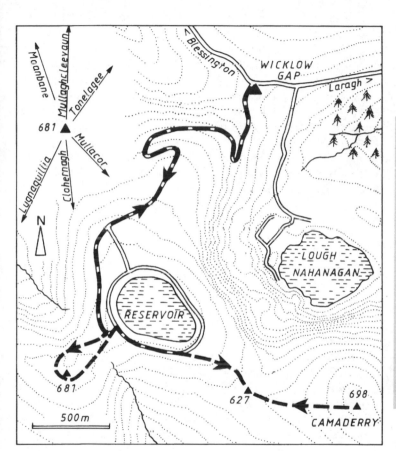

Distance: 5 km
Ascent: 200 m
Time: 2 hours (extra ¾ hour for Camaderry)
Equipment: OS Discovery Sheet 56. Trainers, weather gear.

I've included this walk because it will enable people who cannot cope with rough ground to get to a fine viewpoint in the centre of the Wicklow

Mountains. It is almost all road and more experienced walkers will spurn it, but then they have plenty of other walks within their capabilities.

The level artificial top of Turlough Hill with its projecting control tower is a very obvious landmark from many parts of Wicklow. Constructed nearly thirty years ago, it is the upper reservoir of the Turlough Hill Pumped Storage Scheme, whose lower reservoir is Lough Nahanagan. A pumped storage scheme operates by using electricity generated elsewhere during the small hours to pump water to a high-level reservoir. When everyone switches on the kettle and the stove and the water heater in the morning, water is emptied from the high reservoir and operates turbines to meet the sudden increase in electrical demand. It is the ultimate in 'taking in each other's washing' but is economical because it is much cheaper to keep a fossil fuel generator running all the time than to keep switching it on and off. The ultimate in 'unswitchability' is a nuclear power station, and it may have been the project (fortunately aborted) to build a nuclear station on the Wexford coast that was a factor in the decision to build the Turlough Hill Scheme. The name is modern, coined by the Electricity Supply Board. At least it is apposite; a turlough is a disappearing lake in a limestone area. In dry weather, all the water drains out through cracks in the lake floor, and returns again when the rains come!

Enough of technicality. Walk 35 ('Little' Brockagh) explains how to get to Glendalough. Fork right just before the hotel (still on the R756) which will take you up the wide Glendasan valley. As I write, the surface is excellent — a by-product of the Tour de France in Ireland in 1998. On your left are some spoil heaps, relics of the extensive lead mines which were worked here in the nineteenth century; some of the adits go right through to Glendalough. The ore was taken up to Ballycorus (see Walk 13) for smelting. Soon you see Lough Nahanagan, the lower reservoir. Tradition gave it a monster, but the poor thing must have taken refuge elsewhere now that the water level rises and falls hugely every day. When you reach the Pass at the head of the valley, stop in the car park.

From the car park take the road past the barrier and walk easily uphill. On your left, gloomy cliffs below Turlough Hill overlook Lough Nahanagan; on the right, you look down the valley of the Kings River to the central plains. It was up the Kings River valley and down Glendasan that the pilgrims used to walk to St Kevin's shrine in Glendalough — there is a scheme in progress to make a walking route of it; perhaps it will be ready when you read this. A couple of zigzags (ignore a road on the left) bring you onto the open ridge beside the great earth banks retaining the reservoir; keep going until the road turns back sharply to the reservoir gate.

Take the track which leads off to the right towards a quarry, and when you reach the fence go either left or right (rougher) to the top of the hill (681 m). That's your big walk: now you can enjoy the scenery. Below you is the head of Glendalough backed by the ridge from Mullacor to Conavalla which separates Glendalough from Glenmalure. Beyond is Lugnaquillia, *Log na Coille*, 'Hollow of the Cock', at 925 m the highest mountain in Leinster, with its supporting acolytes, Cannow, Corrigasleggaun, Clohernagh, Carrawaystick. But the pleasure is not just the actual view: it is the feeling of being high up, in the midst of a wilderness, no sign of humankind — as long as you resolutely forget the artificial mound behind you.

If your conscience pricks you at such an easy walk, head off east for 1.5 km along paths through the heather to the top of Camaderry. There you can get the sector of view which the reservoir blocked, from Tonelagee east and south back to 'Lug'.

Jumping to the other extreme: you might push someone in a wheelchair up the road, or — probably more practical — get prior permission from the ESB to take a car up the road.

The return is by the outward route.

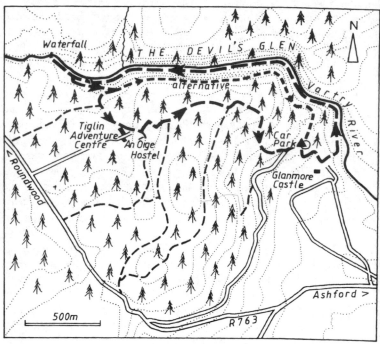

The Devil's Glen

Distance: 5 km
Ascent: 130 m
Time: 1¾ hours (maybe a few minutes longer via Tiglin)
Equipment: OS Discovery Sheet 56. Trainers.

The Devil's Glen is the deep, steep-sided valley — almost a gorge — of the Vartry River below the Vartry Reservoirs (see Walk 31). The walk is entirely on paths, which may be a bit muddy in winter. The highlight of the walk is the waterfall at the head of the valley. The waterfall will be in top form when the reservoirs are full and overflowing, so this is really a walk not to do in summer. Besides, the approach is all through deciduous woods which will look their best in autumn when the leaves are brown, or in winter when the branches are stark and bare, or in spring when the young leaves are unfolding. Note that Sheet 56, while accurate for the roads, does not show the path we walk on the south side of the stream and places the waterfall much too far to the west.

Take the N11, the road to Wicklow and Wexford, as far as Ashford. As you enter the village, there is a road (R763) to the right between a petrol station and a pub, signposted to Roundwood. Almost immediately fork left and after a kilometre fork left again, cross the Vartry by a narrow stone bridge and climb easily past the entrance to Glanmore Castle. At the next fork, go right (for a change) and climb steeply up into forest. After a further kilometre turn sharply right onto a forest road which contours round the hillside, to end in a car park. Below you can glimpse the nineteenth-century crenellations of Glanmore Castle. The castle and all the woodland through which we shall walk once belonged to the Synge family, of whom the most famous member is the writer John Millington Synge. His plays about rural Ireland — particularly the West — produced some of the best writing of the Gaelic Revival. He never lived at Glanmore — his father was a younger brother. The castle and surroundings are still in private hands, but the rest of the Estate is now the property of Coillte, the Irish Forestry Board.

Leave your car and take a path which heads downhill on the right just at the car park entrance. Soon you enter a forest of rhododendron. We think of rhododendron as a shrub, but here there are trunks thicker than your arm, arching over the path to make it a tunnel. Brought in from Asia in the nineteenth century because of its superbly beautiful flowers, it has now become a pest, spreading everywhere and almost impossible to eradicate. The path swings round to the left and then back right, and just when you think it is heading entirely in the wrong direction into the backyard of Glanmore, a white direction arrow on a post sends you to the left. Now all you have to do is follow the path gently downward, with the roar of the river to guide you.

Soon you reach the river's edge, and walk up beside it on a good path. It is a wild stream, tumbling over rocks, all rapids and white water. Down here you are out of rhododendron country into mixed woodland, birch and oak predominating; the pest now is ivy which is clinging to all the trees. You are on the south side of the valley so there is no sun except in high summer, but on a late autumn afternoon you can look across to the steep slopes opposite, where the sun gilds the bare branches and twigs of the birches.

You follow the river bank for half an hour or so until a track joins you from above. There's a marker here which tells you you've been on the 'lower walk' and points you ahead to the waterfall, which you reach in a couple of minutes. The path ends in a viewing point with a fine view of the fall and of a pool below you — a pool which offers a swim on a hot day!

Return as far as the marker and fork right uphill; after a few minutes the main track turns sharply back to the right, while a narrower path goes straight on. There is a choice of return route here. The track leads up to the An Óige Hostel and the Tiglin Adventure Centre (now officially the National Outdoor Training Centre). The hostel was originally an out-farm on the Synge Estate, and the Centre has been built out of some of the barns. They are fine buildings, perhaps the only nineteenth-century architect-designed farm buildings in the country. (This may have been one reason why Synge's grandfather went bankrupt!) To get back to the car park, take the forest road leading east from behind the Centre, and where it swings sharply right, turn left along a narrow path which winds downhill to the east to rejoin the approach road a couple of minutes from the car park. Just before you rejoin the road you pass a modern sculpture in wood, which I can only describe as looking like a gun barrel with insufficient charge to project its missile more than half out of the gun. This route is about 0.5 km longer than the one below.

If you prefer (as I do) to go straight ahead along the side of the valley, you find yourself on a narrow path high above the stream, cut out of the hillside and with sweeping views of the valley. It is not a dull path — at two places there are small bridges, at a third it passes under an arch of rock. The view changes as you walk; the wooded slopes opposite become peppered with small, grey-white rocks and crags. Then you plunge into woodland and at a junction meet two sculptures in wood. These are hung up in small wooden shelter frames. As I approached (and I have to admit my eyesight isn't the best) for one horrific moment they looked like carcasses of animals, but almost immediately I realised they were striking natural tree shapes collected by the artist Kat O'Brien of Canada. Called 'The Seven Shrines', these seven natural sculptures were more attractive than the gun barrel and a couple of other creations further away. Keep straight on past the shrines along the path which swings to the right, through rhododendron country (not unfortunately in flower when I last checked this walk) and back into the corner of the car park.

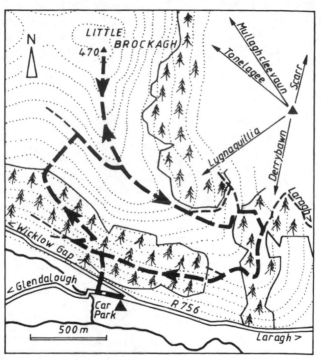

Distance: 6 km
Ascent: 350 m
Time: 2¼ to 2½ hours
Equipment: OS Discovery Sheet 56. Boots or perhaps trainers in summer, weather gear, compass if weather is doubtful.

'Little' Brockagh is the first bump on the ridge that leads over the 'real' Brockagh and on to Tonelagee. It's a fine viewpoint and very easily approached and going on to big brother wouldn't do anything for you except perhaps boost your ego a little. The lower part of the walk is on forest roads, the upper mostly on well-defined tracks with no steep slopes. All very easy going. I only mention the compass because if you happen to be on top in a mist it will start you off downhill in the right direction to

hit the path. Apart from the forest section, all this walk is in the Wicklow National Park. It starts in Glendalough, the most beautiful valley in the Wicklow Mountains. St Kevin came here as a hermit and later, in the ninth century, it became the site of a bishopric, hidden away in this remote valley, away from the danger of Viking raids. On this walk you can look down on all its natural and man-made beauties, and yet avoid the crowds that fill the valley floor — a tourist 'honeypot' if ever there was one!

The walk starts from the car park at the Interpretative Centre or the bus terminus at the Glendalough Hotel. You can get there from Dublin by the St Kevin's bus (one of the few private scheduled buses that still run), or by car. Take the N11 to Kilmacanoge, turn right onto the R755 to Laragh, and beyond the bridge turn right again along the R756 for the short distance to Glendalough.

From the front of the hotel go up the track (Yellow Man marker) to the Wicklow Gap road. Almost opposite cross a stile and climb up, following the Yellow Man to a forest road. He turns right, you turn left and at the next junction turn almost back on your track up a forest road which climbs with one zig to the top of the forest (awaiting replanting at time of writing) and a gate onto the open hillside.

Climb a rather vague path winding up through or beside the deep bracken until you meet heather and, at the same time, a well-defined horizontal track. Turn right (south-east) along the track which rises gently and curves round onto the top of the broad ridge running up to Little Brockagh from the south. Pause for a breather somewhere on this track and get a fine view down onto the Lower and Upper Lakes, and the steep craggy slopes on the far side. In spring or autumn the two lakes reflect the afternoon sun like brilliant mirrors. (Glendalough means the valley of the two lakes.)

Once on the ridge, turn left and climb it easily along a clear path to the summit rocks (470 m). Now the valley is hidden by the swell of the ridge but there are broad distant views all round. The ridge fortunately bends west here so there is a clear view past the 'real' Brockagh to Tonelagee (Walk 32), and the Glendasan valley with Mullaghcleevaun (Walk 30) behind.

For the descent (bearing due south) retrace your upward steps, but instead of turning off the ridge where you joined it on the ascent, continue down its broad crest. This is a delightful stretch: easy walking, gentle descent, good views, I can't think of anywhere better to be on a sunny day with a bit of breeze. It's popular with sheep too and they gaze resentfully at you before seeming to shrug their shoulders and move away at your approach. You pass a sheep fold, fork right and follow the track as it swings round to the left, passing a notice forbidding hunting. Walls and fields appear; go through a small gate and down a steep little path to a forest road. Turn right and descend until you come to a junction where you turn right again, picking up the yellow Walking Man symbols of the Wicklow Way. You are on a little-used road through mature forest, soft underfoot. It descends, passes through a fence, and deteriorates to a rocky track which climbs through young trees almost smothered by gorse, to a high point where once again the view of Glendalough's lakes and crags opens up. (Even when the trees grow, Coillte, the Irish Forestry Board, will almost certainly leave a small gap to maintain this view.) The track descends, crosses another fence into mature forest and becomes a real forest road again. A few minutes along the road the Yellow Man points the way down the hill, back to your transport or the bar of the Glendalough Hotel — or both.

If you haven't been in Glendalough before, take time to visit the Interpretative Centre beside the car park and the ruins of the monastic settlement. If you still have an hour to spare, walk up the far side of the river and climb to Poulanass Waterfall, a bright, white cataract hidden in the wood. Details of this walk will be found in the description of Walk 36, Derrybawn Mountain.

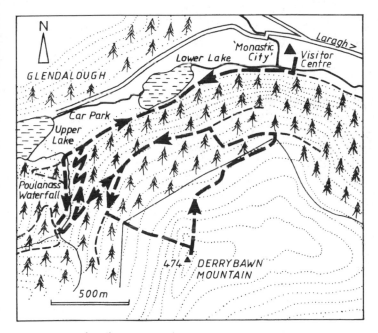

Distance: 7.5 km (longest route)
Ascent: 300 m
Time: 3 hours (longest route)
Equipment: OS Discovery Sheet 56. Boots, weather gear, sticks useful.

I went to check this walk on a beautiful sunny day in late September. When I found the car park bulging with what seemed like half the population of Dublin — walking, picnicking and splashing in the river — I nearly went home. But Glendalough is beautiful enough to rise above its popularity and I spent a most enjoyable afternoon walking to Derrybawn. This is a walk of two halves: good paths in the woods, steep little tracks across the open ground above. If you are inexperienced, you should have sampled a few other walks in the book before trying this one. All the same it's not hard.

You start at the car park at the Glendalough Visitor Centre — see Walk 35 ('Little' Brockagh) for the approach. Follow the signboards for 'Monastic City' and the Wicklow Way Walking Man across the bridge over the river and turn right along the 'Green Road', a delightful, broad track along the south side of the Glendalough valley, with a varied mixed forest (oak and birch predominate) rising steeply on your left and the 'Monastic City' on your right. You should definitely visit this, with its early churches and round tower — perhaps on the way back? Soon you pass the Lower Lake, with its reed beds glimpsed through the trees, and twenty minutes or so will bring you to more open ground and another busy car park at the foot of the Upper Lake.

(You could also start from here, and save a good forty minutes coming and going, but the Green Road is so attractive that it shouldn't be missed. Also the road between the two car parks is narrow and very busy, and as I write the upper car park costs £1.50 at weekends while the lower one is free!)

Pass the Information Centre and turn left at the sign at the bridge for Poulanass Waterfall (you need have no worries about crossing this bridge — it carries a sign pronouncing it safe for fifteen-tonne loads!). Once across the bridge follow the Yellow Man up the stepped path which keeps near the stream and gives close views of the Poulanass Waterfall, where the stream, squeezed between rocks, drops white and foaming in a series of small cataracts. The path rejoins the forest road and very soon you turn left (still with the Yellow Man) over a bridge, and almost immediately fork right uphill (take note of this junction: the left fork is your homeward route).

The forest road climbs easily through open conifer woodland, and then turns sharp right (Walking Man) along another forest road. The going gets tougher soon after this junction; the frail may prefer not to make this turn, but to go straight on for 100 m or so to a seat and viewpoint up the valley, there to await the others. There's an even better viewpoint in my opinion, down over the Lower Lake and monastic ruins, a few metres further along — but no seat!

For those who continue, there are tantalisingly beautiful glimpses through the trees of the Upper Lake and the crags which enclose it. The road rises slightly, and as it begins to descend again, a narrow path appears on the left, climbing steeply. This takes you up to the edge of the forest at a corner. Climb the stile and follow the narrow path through deep heather. Now Derrybawn is in full view, with the path clear to see, heading nearly straight to the ridge. Steep, but not difficult! Once on the ridge, turn right and a couple of minutes brings you to the cairn on Derrybawn's summit (474 m). It's a fine viewpoint, high enough to look over the trees, with only higher ground blocking the view to the south. Look up Glendalough; beyond the Upper Lake you will see the tailings and spoil heaps of the extensive lead mines which were worked in the nineteenth century. There are long adits, some of which go right through to Glendasan. The remotest mine was nicknamed 'Van Diemen's Land', the original name of Tasmania, a penal colony to which many Irishmen were transported!

You can return to the forest road by the route of ascent, or be a little more adventurous. Where your upward path reached the ridge, keep straight on over a small bump and then descend, bearing a little right by a very vague path through heather. Even if you lose the path you can see it ahead cutting clearly through bracken, and aim for that. Soon the path joins an old paved track which you follow, rising a little, into a corner of the wood and onto a path which brings you very quickly to a forest road. Turn left along this. The next bit poses the only difficulty. You have to drop down to the forest road out of sight below you. There are little paths, but so indistinct that I can't easily advise you, except to say that because it is felled or open forest, you can easily see your way. You are better in the forest; the felled areas have branches hidden in the grass to trip the unwary. Once on the lower road, your troubles are over.

Stride out to the left along the level road, pick up your frail companions (if any!) at the viewpoint seat and continue down the upward route to the junction before the bridge. Turn sharp right along a forest road which soon narrows to a path which zigzags down beside the Poulanass stream opposite your upward route. This is a delightful path; on my walk for this guide I found myself in the midst of yellow gorse, deep purple heather and the bright red berries of the mountain ash, backed by birch trees just beginning to turn autumn brown. Then there are steep little side paths which will bring you close to the stream, more excitingly than the fenced path on the far side. One and a half 'Zs' later you pass through a kissing gate back onto the Green Road. All that remains is a gentle stroll back to hotel or car park which, don't forget, closes at 6 p.m.

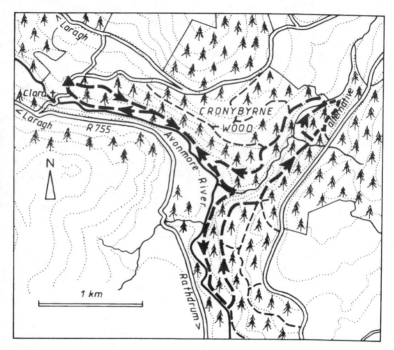

Distance: 8 km
Ascent: 100 m
Time: 2½ hours
Equipment: OS Discovery Sheet 56. Trainers.

I came upon this walk almost by chance. I planned a walk up Trooperstown Hill from the woods above the Avonmore River, and looking at the map wondered if a walk through the woods beside the Avonmore might be more attractive. It was! I walked it on a sunny November day, when the birch and oak trees were at their brightest red and russet. After overnight heavy rain the river swirled past, turgid and noisy. Of course I can't promise you the same conditions, but I do recommend the autumn! (I had actually been there several times before, but I had been orienteering, when you have no time to appreciate your surroundings!)

From Dublin take the N11 to Kilmacanoge, turn right on the R755 and continue through Roundwood and Laragh towards Rathdrum. Just 5.3 km beyond Laragh, mostly through deciduous woodland above the Avonmore, turn sharply left downhill to the very attractive little hamlet of Clara. This must be the smallest hamlet in Ireland: a couple of houses, a bridge and a church. Cross the bridge and climb the hill to a forest entrance on the right, where you park.

Enter the forest and walk the track, first under a nearly closed canopy and then in a more open woodland of birches, fine old oaks, tall pines and holly, with a view down to the Avonmore River and valley. Here the autumn colours were at their best, with the green of the tall pine trees providing a background to the autumn colours of the oak and birch.

The track now descends to the river; note a junction left — that is where you will emerge on your return journey. The track narrows to a path — no vehicles have been here for a long time — crosses a tributary by an old stone bridge and continues along the flat strip between the river and a steep, high bank. The rapids along here are favoured by canoeists — you may well see a group enjoying themselves.

The whole area belongs to Coillte, the Irish Forestry Board, but mostly they have left the old deciduous forest and have even planted more birch trees. In one place there is a flat re-entrant with a mass of young birches, their twigs so massed that at a distance it looks like a brown mist.

About fifteen minutes from the bridge you come to a junction; turn left and take the path which rises gently off the valley floor and swings away from the river, passing two junctions to reach an open area. On the far side there is a wall of conifers, tall and straight like a regiment of Prussian Guards. Before you reach these trees there is a multiple junction where you again fork left, keeping along the edge of the cleared area. Soon you are back in the trees — this time planted conifers. Just beyond an open stretch on your right (nearly 1 km from the junction), you cross a streamlet with a wall running downhill beyond it. Leave the track and walk through the trees beside the wall. There's no path, but if you follow the line of planting a little beyond the wall it is quite easy going. You meet an abandoned track sloping down to your left back towards the wall.

Follow it down and round as it swings away again and then go straight down to a path beside a stream — the tributary which you crossed early on. Follow this path upstream to the right, past a rocky bluff, until you meet a big boulder beside the path, and a narrow path to the left which brings you across the stream. (If you miss the streamlet and wall, don't worry, continue along the forest track, take two left turns and you arrive at the big boulder from the other direction; it's easier, but longer.)

Now you are really on your way home. The narrow path climbs out of the valley and meets a forest road in open woodland. Two left turns bring you back to your outward track. Follow it until, where the wood closes in, a left fork leads you down to the river. The path gets narrower and less distinct until you think it will disappear, but winding among the bushes and trees of the river bank it keeps on and then climbs up to meet the public road between Clara and the forest entrance. Turn right and in a very few minutes you'll be back at the car.

Return to Laragh by the way you came, or continue up the hill, turn sharp left and get another feast of autumn colours along a byroad which rejoins the R755 just below Laragh, where there is plenty of refreshment to be found, alcoholic and otherwise.

38.  Deputy's Pass

Distance: 2.5 km
Ascent: 40 m
Time: ¾ hour
Equipment: OS Discovery Sheet 56 (62 would be useful — the walk is on the edge of 56). Trainers — but it may be muddy.

Looking at the map of Wicklow, I have been intrigued for years by the name Deputy's Pass; it must obviously, I felt, refer to some historical happening, probably a battle that the Wicklowmen won over the English. Until this year I had never visited it; too short, not interesting enough. In fact I would never have thought of it for this book if an unconnected task had not taken me there last summer. Short it is, but it is a pleasant woodland stroll, through mature, deciduous forest, part forest track, part narrow path, with one open section. It is entirely within the Nature Reserve (a Reserve because of its fine oak trees) shown on the OS map.

Like so many of these narrow gaps in the hills in Wicklow, the Pass is a glacial overflow channel through which there now runs a small stream, with the grandiose name of Potters River. It is an obvious low-level route between South Wicklow and the broad Glenealy valley, probably a link in the path that pilgrims would have taken from the south-east on their way to St Kevin's shrine in Glendalough.

A very little research produced some answers to the origin of the name, which again relates to its value as a pass through the hills. Curtis's *History of Ireland* states: 'in 1580 in the lonely pass of Glenmalure Fiach MacHugh O'Byrne gave a complete overthrow to the forces of the Deputy, Lord Grey de Wilton'. Then in 1599, during the Earl of Essex's pathetic attempts to subdue Ireland (which culminated in his precipitate return to England and beheading), there was definitely a battle in the Pass, when Felim and Redmond O'Byrne, sons of Fiach MacHugh, defeated Sir Henry Harrington, Seneschal of Wicklow. Such a narrow pass between high wooded slopes is a perfect place for an ambush, and it would be surprising if there were not several battles there. The O'Byrnes, secure in their fastnesses in the Wicklow Mountains, were always a serious threat to the Pale, the area round Dublin where English law prevailed.

From Dublin take the Wexford road (N11) through Ashford and Rathnew, and where it turns sharp left under a railway bridge, continue straight on along the R752 through Glenealy and under another railway bridge. Take the left turn about 0.5 km beyond the bridge and stop after about another 0.5 km in a car park (not marked on OS map). This is a pleasant picnic spot with the stream tinkling beside the tables. You could also reach the turn-off from the R752 by the bus from Dublin to Rathdrum.

The walk starts up the track to the left of the picnic area, climbing gently through mature mixed wood, and then dropping a little to a junction where you fork left. This brings you into an open area where the track passes between long grass and meadow flowers past an old ruin. Savour this open section with its views, for the rest of the walk you are in woodland. Once more in woodland the track rises again to a four-way junction — continue straight on. The character of the wood changes: trees are smaller, and high shrubs and gorse close in to leave a narrow path. After a few hundred metres it opens out again into fine, high woodland of mature trees, swinging rightward and descending gently back to the picnic area.

If you feel this is a long way to come for such a short stroll, and have a car, you might like to follow those putative pilgrims I mentioned and return to Dublin via Glendalough. Just on the Glenealy side of the railway bridge turn left up a delightful wooded valley. The second turn left off this road and a straight-on at a rather complicated crossroads a kilometre or so later, takes you onto a road through the woods high above the Avonmore River to Laragh and the Dublin road — or a short diversion up to Glendalough. In autumn, when the leaves are turning, the colours — greens, russets, reds — along this Avonmore drive should not be missed.

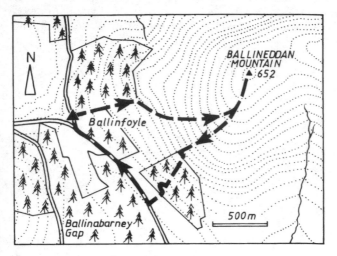

Distance: 4.5 km (or 4 km returning same way)
Ascent: 360 m
Time: 2 to 2¼ hours
Equipment: OS Discovery Sheet 56 and (useful but not absolutely necessary), Sheet 62. Boots, weather gear, compass if weather is doubtful, sticks useful.

There is no way that Lugnaquillia (925 m, Log na Coille, Hollow of the Cock), the highest mountain in Leinster and one of only fourteen 'Munros' (mountains exceeding 3,000 ft [915 m] — see Walk 15) in all Ireland, could be included in our short walks. However, you can get a toehold on it by climbing Ballineddan Mountain (Sliabh Bhaile an Fheadáin, Mountain of the Village of the Small Stream), its most western outlier. Though involving a fairly steep ascent partly on untracked grass and heather, Ballineddan lies right on the edge of the Wicklow Mountains and provides wide views of the inland plains, as well as a close-up of Lugnaquillia.

From Dublin take the N81 through Blessington; about 22 km beyond Blessington, turn left at a crossroads, signposted to the

Dwyer-McAllister Cottage. This road brings you, after about 5 km, to Knockanarrigan crossroads. Turn right (signposted Aughavannagh), and, still following Dwyer-McAllister signs, fork sharp right then left; continuing past the Cottage, keep left at the next fork where a sign announces Ballinabarney Gap. After 4.5 km from Knockanarrigan there is a junction (Ballinfoyle on Sheet 56) with a military warning notice — the area further north is an Army firing range, but this walk does not go near the range and the warnings can be ignored. Take the road to the left and park on the wide verge on the left.

Less than 100 m from the junction a gate on the right leads to a rough track winding up the wide gap between two forestry plantations. Soon another gate leads to a distinct path, heading uphill alongside the wall and fence marking the edge of the forestry on the left; towards the top, the trees are at present very small and may not obviously be a forest. At the top of the forestry where the fence turns away north (left) the path veers right and slants uphill for a while before degenerating into a sheep path traversing the hillside southward. At this point it is time to leave the path; pick any reasonable-looking line and head straight up the slope, out of the heather and up over tussocky grass, mostly dry underfoot and quite reasonable going though steep. Eventually the slope eases off and another path appears running along just off the crest of the broad, rounded southern ridge of Ballineddan. Turn left on this; a gentle climb brings one to the small cairn marking the summit (652 m).

The broad, bare, grassy summit offers no shelter, and in mist and wind it can be very bleak and cold. On either a fine day in summer with larks singing, or on a calm, sunny winter day with snow on the higher hills, it can be idyllic. To the east the path continues across a short dip and on over Slievemaan. Lugnaquillia can be seen looming behind, sometimes hidden in dark clouds even when Ballineddan is clear, often snow-covered in winter. To the west and south are wide views over the Glen of Imaal and the flat lowlands beyond, interrupted only by the bulk of Keadeen Mountain (Walk 40).

To descend, you have two options. Firstly, you can reverse the route, the main difficulty being choosing where to leave the ridge path. In bad visibility a compass bearing due west from the summit will bring you to the young forest just north of the path.

An alternative route (and easier navigationally) is to follow the path down the ridge. This descends gently for a while, then the slope steepens dramatically and a high dry-stone wall appears to guide the path down to a forest. Turn left along the top of the forest for 35 m, to find an old moss-covered stone wall leading down into the forest, which at the time of writing is mature and fairly easy going underfoot. Follow the wall as it slants leftward and down until you reach a forest road near the bottom of the forest. Go downhill on this road as it leads through a gate, across a field, and through another gate to the tarmac road, and turn right to get to the start 1 km along the road.

For rehydration in summer or hot whiskey in winter, return to Knockanarrigan, turn right and drive for 2 km to reach the pub at Seskin much frequented by walkers.

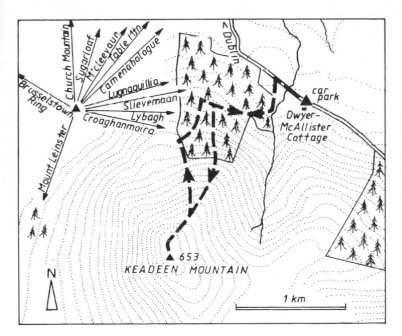

Distance: 5 km
Ascent: 450 m
Time: 2½ to 3 hours
Equipment: OS Discovery Sheet 56 and (useful but not absolutely necessary) Sheet 62. Boots, weather gear, compass if weather is doubtful, sticks useful.

Keadeen is an isolated south-west outpost of the Wicklow Mountains, overlooking the Glen of Imaal which is backed by the mass of Lugnaquillia. The typical, flat summit area is surrounded on all sides except to the south by unusually steep slopes, and this walk involves some steep, uphill climbs and some rough ground in places. However, the very steepness means the views are quite spectacular. There are few paths on this walk so boots are essential.

From Dublin take the N81; about 22 km south of Blessington, turn left, following signs for Knockanarrigan and the Dwyer-McAllister Cottage. After 5 km you come to the tiny village of Knockanarrigan — turn right here (signposted Aughavannagh and Dwyer-McAllister Cottage), and, following the signs for the Cottage, fork sharp right, then left, and park in the car park opposite the Cottage about a mile from Knockanarrigan. The fame of the Cottage takes us back to the years after the 1798 Rebellion, when British soldiers were still trying to catch Michael Dwyer. He was trapped in the Cottage, but Sam McAllister stepped out in his place and was shot while Dwyer escaped. Walk back (westward) for 200 m on the road past a house, to a gate on the left, which leads to a (literally) green road — a grass-covered track. Follow this as it goes through more gates, veers right and enters a forest, climbing gently.

Continue along the track to a huge turning circle. Here it is time to plunge into the forest on the left and gain some height. A broken-down, moss-covered wall runs up the hill marking the change from mature forest to the younger and at present almost impenetrable trees to the east. Keep this wall to your right, and though in places you may have to dodge fallen trees, with a little care a reasonable way can be found directly up the gradually steepening slope to the top of the forest. Here there is a stile to cross the fence. At 400 m the Glen of Imaal already seems far below, but in front is still a steep, heather-covered slope to surmount. Climb straight upward, and after a while the slope becomes a little less steep and mainly grassy, making it easier going up to a false summit. Just below this, some rocks show the upper end of an old ruined but substantial wall, a useful feature for the descent.

Beyond the very convincing false summit you will see yet more grassy and heathery slopes, less steep than those below; then suddenly a fence, a stone wall, and a very large cairn mark the top. The summit is a long, flat area, with the highest point at the southern end marked by a trig. pillar (653 m), but far more interesting at the north end is the cairn, the remains of a large structure which may have contained a passage grave. With imagination, a few hollows in the stone could be construed to be the result of the roof of the almost north-pointing passage falling in. Many of the stones have been recycled to build a stone wall but plenty are left to indicate the impressive size of the original structure. This is a better place to shelter from the usual wind and look around than the exposed trig. point.

Looking north across the Glen of Imaal, the first hill to the right is Church Mountain. Moving around the skyline, the mountains overlooking the glen are the Sugar Loaf, Lobawn, Table Mountain (with Mullaghcleevaun behind), then comes the great bulk of the main Lugnaquillia massif — Camenabologue, Cannow, 'Lug' itself, Slievemaan and Lybagh with the point of Croaghanmoira beyond. To the south-east are the rolling hills of Wexford and South Wicklow while to the south the Blackstairs Mountains are plain, with the television mast on top of Mount Leinster. The Central Plain fades into the distance to the west but much closer, almost at your feet, is yet another prehistoric structure, the Brusselstown Ring, a great stone wall girdling a hilltop.

You can return by the same route, or for variety descend to the false summit, find the end of the ruined wall and follow it down. After a while the ground flattens out and becomes wetter; continue along the wall now with young forest to the right until just before a fence a stile leads onto a track leading into the forest. This can be followed down to a junction with another track — turn right here and you arrive out in the turning circle. (In mist it may be difficult to find the right direction, but if it becomes necessary it is possible to descend keeping the fence to one's left. Some parts are steep, and lower down it becomes quite wet. When you meet another fence turn right along it to yet another fence junction. To the right here, a short way uphill is a track leading into the forest.)

The pub to go to in the Glen of Imaal is undoubtedly in Seskin — turn right in Knockanarrigan. Nearly any weekend you will find walkers congregating there, down from 'Lug' or any of the mountains you could see from Keadeen.

Park Walks

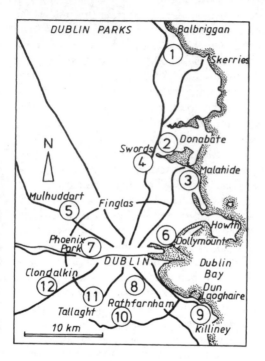

We are fortunate in the Dublin area to have some very fine parks in which can be found delightful and varied short walks. I am not going to list every public green space in Dublin City and adjoining counties but here is a selection of the most interesting with a few notes on what you may find. I will not, in general, describe any itineraries because these parks are really just places to wander at will. Most of them have the advantage that there is something to interest all ages — you can bring granny as well as the six-year-old.

Consult the Parks Division of the relevant Local Authority for more information, such as opening hours etc. (you will find them in the telephone directory). Some booklets are available. Note that the opening hours of the houses are generally more restricted than the park opening hours. All these parks are reasonably accessible by public transport, but you should always consult the timetable before you set out — some services are quite infrequent.

All the parks except Ardgillan and Newbridge can be found on the OS Dublin Street Guide.

Fingal County

1. Ardgillan Castle
Location: On the coast road between Skerries and Balbriggan.
Access: Number 33 bus from Eden Quay (quite a long journey — 1¾ hours). By car, take the Belfast road (N1), turn off onto the R127 through Lusk and you will find good road signs to lead you to the car parks.

Ardgillan Castle was the home of the Taylor family whose ancestor came to Ireland as Deputy Surveyor to William Petty who made the 'Down' Survey in the 1650s. His grandson built the first house here in the early eighteenth century; the turrets and other appurtenances of a castle were added in Victorian times. The Castle and park were sold to Dublin County Council in 1981. The Castle is open and contains a fine selection of period furniture. Maps of the Down Survey are on show and there is a coffee shop.

The entrance from the bus is by a footbridge over the railway from the Skerries–Balbriggan road. The railway, built in the 1840s, cut off the family's access to the sea, and the railway company had to build this access to the beach, now called the 'Lady's Stairs'.

As well as the Castle you will find woodland walks, a walled garden and a rose garden, and great views all the way round from the Mourne Mountains to Lambay.

2. Newbridge Demesne
Location: Just west of Donabate.
Access: Number 33B bus passing the entrance, or rail to Donabate from Connolly Station. By car to the entrance off the N1, north of Swords.

The Estate belonged to the Cobbes, who, like many great Anglo-Irish families, fell on hard times. It was bought by Dublin County Council and opened in 1986. Newbridge House, built by Archbishop Cobbe, is a typical eighteenth-century country house. It is open to the public, and much fine period furniture and works of art, on loan from the Cobbe family, are on display. The courtyard has been restored and opened as a museum of late eighteenth-century rural life. There is a traditional farm with small animals, much patronised by primary-school parties. The gardens, probably laid out by Charles Frizell, are a very good example of eighteenth-century garden design.

Pleasant walks in the wood and parkland, birdlife, football area, and coffee shop in the Courtyard.

3. Malahide Castle
Location: Just outside Malahide, off the Dublin road.
Access: Numbers 32A and 42 buses from Talbot Street. Train from Connolly to Malahide. By car, turn right off the Malahide road (R107) a kilometre or so before the town.

The Castle and Estate belonged to the Talbot family from 1185, when the lands were granted to them by Henry II, until 1977; then, after the death of Milo Talbot who was responsible for creating the Botanic Gardens, it was bought by Dublin County Council. Very little remains of the original castle; over the centuries it was transformed into a comfortable country house.

The Castle is now open to the public and is worth visiting. Adjoining the Castle are both a very sophisticated model railway layout in the Railway Museum, and the internationally known Talbot Botanical Gardens with over five thousand species mainly from the southern hemisphere.

Other facilities include walks, par 3 golf, pitch and putt, tennis and football, a children's playground, and a coffee shop and restaurant in the Castle.

4. Ward River Linear Park
See Walk 2.

5. Tolka Valley Park
Location: Mulhuddart to Finglas South.
Access: Lots of buses!

The sections of park along the Tolka Valley will soon form a fine linear walk. Check with Finglas County Council for developments!

Dublin Corporation

6. St Anne's Park
Location: Between Dollymount on the coast road to Howth (James Larkin Road) and Killester.
Access: Number 130 bus to Dollymount; Numbers 29A, 31 and 32 to Killester and Raheny.

There are many small parks within the Corporation area but this is the only important one for which it is responsible. Originally a demesne belonging to the Guinness family, it was developed chiefly by Arthur Guinness, later Lord Ardilaun, but after the death of his widow in 1925 it lay empty until bought by the Corporation in 1939. The house was demolished in the late 1960s. Under the recent, more enlightened, policies of the Corporation it might have been saved.

The Park is perhaps known best for its Rose Garden, but there are also some pleasant parkland and woodland walks where you may come upon a Folly — there are several in the Park.

7. Phoenix Park
Location: Between Parkgate, Chapelizod and Castleknock.
Access: Numbers 25, 26, 51 and 66 buses along the south side; number 37 bus along the north side.

Although within the Corporation boundary, Phoenix Park, one of the largest urban parks in the world (over 700 hectares), is managed by the Office of Public Works. The curious name 'Phoenix' is a corruption of the Irish *fionn uisce*, 'fair' or 'clear' water, referring it seems to a spring.

The residence of the Viceroy had been in the Park since the early seventeenth century, although it only grew to its present size by the nineteenth century. The Viceroy's residence is now Áras an Uachtaráin, the residence of the President. The Park also includes the residence of the American Ambassador, the Zoo, a hospital and the Ordnance Survey, but this still leaves plenty of room for open parkland and woodland where a sizeable herd of deer roams freely. My favourite area for walking is along the southern slopes between the Islandbridge Gate and the Knockmaroon Gate, including the Furry Glen.

In the north-west corner there is an Interpretative Centre and coffee shop beside the old Ashtown Castle.

8. The Dodder Valley Path

Since it is strictly urban, and has often been described elsewhere, I have not included the Dodder among my walks. However, it makes a good walk between Clonskeagh and Templeogue, most of it on paths through a linear park, and including a possible diversion into Bushy Park. You can join or leave the path at any of the major bridges, all of which have bus routes into the centre of the city.

Dun Laoghaire–Rathdown County

9. Killiney Hill Park
See Walk 8.

10. Marlay Park
Location: Rathfarnham, between Grange Road and College Road.
Access: Number 47B bus from Hawkins Street.

Another park formed from an old demesne which was laid out mainly by the La Touche family in the eighteenth century. The house is being restored and has not yet been opened to the public, but the courtyard close by is now a Craft Centre, including a coffee shop and craft shops where stained glass, leather, copper and other handcrafted gifts can be bought.

The Wicklow Way, a waymarked long-distance walk, starts here. Its route can be seen on the map board in the car park, and the first few hundred metres of the Way can be followed through the Park, using the waymarks which feature a yellow walking figure.

There are plenty of facilities in the Park: woodland walks with streams, waterfalls, lakes and wildfowl, a model railway on which children can ride, par 3 golf, a BMX track, permanent orienteering courses, tennis courts, football and cricket pitches.

The southern edge of the Park is currently a mess and is likely to remain so for at least two years during construction of the Southern Cross motorway.

South Dublin County

11. Tymon Park
Location: Tallaght, squeezed between the Tallaght bypass and the M50.
Access: Numbers 15A, 54A and 150 buses on Wellington Road; numbers 50, 77 and 77A on Greenhills Road.

This is an unlikely spot for a park, bisected by the M50 motorway, but there are attractive paths and a stream which has been landscaped to make small lakes and waterfalls. It is still being developed.

12. Corkagh Demesne
Location: Clondalkin, St John's Road.
Access: Numbers 68 and 68A buses.

Another unexpected park in the middle of housing estates in South County Dublin. The house was demolished by a developer and the whole area was in danger, but the Council has rescued it and created a pleasant park with the Camac River flowing through it.

There are many fine trees, and there is an arboretum of tree species from all the countries to which people emigrated during the Famine. A successful effort has been made to maintain a natural habitat for wildlife; there is a wildflower meadow, and more than fifty bird species have been seen as well as many small mammals.

There is a children's playground and a picnic area.

Bibliography

There are a number of books which will enhance your enjoyment of these walks. Most important is *The Neighbourhood of Dublin*, Weston St J. Joyce, which I have quoted quite often. Although first published in 1912 (reprinted, Dublin 1971) it is still an interesting source of historical information, and an index to the enormous changes in Dublin during eighty years.

Other books which we have consulted and which you may find are good background reading include the following:

Conlin, Stephen and de Courcy, John, *Anna Liffey*, Dublin 1988.
Delany, Ruth, *The Royal Canal*, Dublin 1992.
Delany, Ruth, *The Grand Canal*, Dublin 1995.
Harbison, Peter, *National Monuments of Ireland*, Dublin 1992.
Healy, Elizabeth (ed.), *The Book of the Liffey*, Dublin 1988.
Herity, Michael, *Irish Passage Graves*, Dublin 1974.
Hutchinson, Clive, *Birds of Dublin and Wicklow*, Dublin 1975.
Jeffrey, D.W. (ed.), *North Bull Island*, Dublin 1977.
The Flora of County Dublin, Dublin Field Naturalists Club, Dublin 1998.
The Open Forest, Coillte, Dublin n.d.
The Parks of Fingal, Fingal County Council n.d.

If you want longer walks in Dublin, Wicklow and the southeast, try *Walk Guide East of Ireland*, Jean Boydell, David Herman, Miriam Joyce McCarthy, Dublin 1997.

If the waterside takes your fancy, try *Irish Waterside Walks*, Michael Fewer, Dublin 1997, which describes such walks all round the country, including some around Dublin which aren't in this book.

You will also find ideas for walks around Dublin in the books of David Herman, Christopher Moriarty and Pat Liddy.